I0153462

Mr. Huston/
Mr. North:

Mr. Huston/ Mr. North:

Life, Death, and Making John Huston's Last Film

by Nat Segaloff

BearManor Media

2015

© 1987, 2014 by Nat Segaloff. All rights reserved. Except for brief passages in published reviews, no part of this book may be reproduced, converted, or transmitted in any form by any information storage and retrieval system without permission in writing from the author and with appropriate credit to the author, source, and publisher.

Portions of this work appeared previously in *The Boston Herald*, which purchased first North American publication rights from the Author under prevailing freelance practices, and in the author's *Final Cuts: The Last Films of 50 Great Directors* (BearManor Media, 2013). Pages from *The Boston Herald* are reproduced courtesy of *The Boston Herald*.

Published by BearManor Media and printed in the United States of America.
P. O. Box 71426, Albany, GA 31708
www.BearManorMedia.com

Library of Congress Cataloging-in-Publication Data: 2015911133
Segaloff, Nat, 1948 -
        Mr. Huston/Mr. North: Life, Death, and Making John Huston's Last Film /

ISBN: 978-1-59393-835-2

Excerpts from non-authorial interviews, letters, and other material appear under a Fair Use Rights claim of U.S. Copyright Law, Title 17, U.S.C. with copyrights reserved by their respective rights holders. Many designations used by manufacturers to distinguish their products (such as Oscar®, Academy Award®, and Steadicam®) are claimed as trademarks or service marks. Where those designations appear in this book and the publisher was aware of such a claim, the designations contain the symbols ®, SM, or ™ on their initial appearance. Any omission of these symbols is purely accidental and is not intended as an infringement.

"OSCAR®," "OSCARS®," "ACADEMY AWARD®," "ACADEMY AWARDS®," "OSCAR NIGHT®," "A.M.P.A.S.®" and the federally registered "Oscar" design mark are registered and copyrighted by the Academy of Motion Picture Arts and Sciences.

Photographs from *Mr. North* by Anthony K. (Kal) Roberts.

Disclaimer: Nothing herein implies that this book is authorized by or connected with the makers or owners of *Mr. North*. Everyone quoted in this book was advised at the time of the interview that he or she was on the record. Although Heritage Entertainment provided full access to their production, at no time did they have any influence or control, either financial or editorial, in what I wrote for *The Boston Herald* or what appears in this book.

Cover and Book design by John Teehan
Cover photograph of The Breakers by Jeanpaul Ferro

For the Lion
and his Pride
and
Ernest (Ernie) Anderson

Table of Contents

Introduction &
Acknowledgments

Mr. *North* was an ordinary film made under extraordinary circumstances. Modest of budget, humble of ambition, and pleasant of purpose, it was intended, first, as light entertainment, and, second, as a means by which a young director could get a foothold on a career. Inasmuch as the young director was the son of a very well-known older director, the father prevailed upon his movie star friends to help him give his son a jumpstart into feature filmmaking. What nobody anticipated was that the director-father would become critically ill just as filming started and that his struggle to postpone death would haunt every moment of what was supposed to be a romantic adventure set in a recent fairy-tale past.

The old director was John Huston, and the events surrounding what became the last film he would ever work on would color the memories of all who shared it, not the least of whom were his family, who started their filmmaking adventure with the highest of hopes, and ended it in grief. This book tells that story.

John Huston was a legend whose life rivaled any of his films. *The African Queen, The Treasure of the Sierra Madre, The Maltese Falcon, Beat the Devil, Moulin Rouge, The Man Who Would Be King, Under the Volcano, Prizzi's Honor, The Red Badge of Courage, Fat City, The Asphalt Jungle, Wise Blood, The Dead,* and a dozen other titles carried his bravura stamp. Even those that didn't quite work, or that he may have done purely for the money—*Victory, Phobia, Casino Royale, The Bible* and, of course, *Annie*—still showed strengths, albeit at times elusive.

Ironically, one of the truest Huston portraits was rendered in a film he didn't make: *White Hunter, Black Heart* (1990). Based on Peter Viertel's 1953 *roman à clef* about making *The African Queen* in the then Belgian Congo in 1951, it starred Clint Eastwood as a Huston-esque director who was more interested in shooting a bull elephant than the movie. Like Huston, Eastwood strutted in boots, chewed on a cigar, and acted soft-spoken and courtly as he manipulated those around him with playful delight. But, of course, Eastwood was not Huston, even though—and this is said only for people who find such things noteworthy—each of them directed westerns with similar titles: Huston, in 1960, *The Unforgiven*, and Eastwood, in 1992, *Unforgiven*. They were both also tall men and brilliant filmmakers.

Even when his health failed, Huston the man did not. Toward the end, he was still Huston. He was confined to a wheelchair and tethered to an oxygen canister that allowed him to breathe as much as his emphysema-wracked body would allow. Surrounded by a retinue, he not only directed his life, it soon became clear that he directed his death.

In July of 1987, Ernie Anderson, Huston's longtime friend and stalwart press agent ("Don't call me a publicist!" he would bark), approached my editor at *The Boston Herald* with an enticing idea: Why not assign a reporter to the filming of *Mr. North*, a movie based on Thornton Wilder's late-in-life novel *Theophilus North*? The picture was just about to get underway in Newport, Rhode Island, fabled summer resort of the fabulously wealthy. Realizing what a perfect chance this would be for the tabloid to have exclusive, behind-the-scenes stories about well-known stars, visiting celebrities, society doyens, and movie magic, the *Herald* did just what any alert, aggressive, competitive, far-sighted newspaper would do.

They turned him down.

That is when Ernie went to work on them. "It'll be a journalistic coup," he pitched. "You get to spend the summer at Newport at the height of the season. For free! And you get to mix with movie folks who actually want you on the set and won't have their bodyguards chase you off!" (He didn't mention, of course, that the massive ongoing publicity would make him a hero.)

"No," said my editor. "We don't have the space to run daily stories."

If he put his mind to it, Ernie Anderson could get the B'nai B'rith to sponsor a ham banquet. He was a man who not only would not take "no," but knew whom to call who could say "yes." Proud of his profession, he had been around long enough to know when "no" meant "I'll think about it," and "I'll think about it" meant "yes."

Within three days, Ernie got the *Herald* editors to say, "I'll think about it."

By the next day, they said, "yes."

Then they discovered that no staff reporter would take the assignment.

"Are you nuts?" the editor squawked as each of his writers turned him down. "You get to spend the summer at Newport at the height of the season. For free! And you get to mix with movie folks who actually want you on the set and won't have their bodyguards chase you off!"

"No," each of them said. They would not even "think it over."

That is when the editor called in The Freelancer.[1]

What is a Freelancer?

With the abolishment of slavery in America, Freelancers may be the country's sole remaining indentured servants (with legislative aides and talent agency assistants tying for a close second). In journalism, Freelancers work on a piece-by-piece basis with no job security, are paid lower fees than staff writers, get no fringe benefits, have to pay self-employment tax, and have little control over how their copy is edited. They are often prevented by the union that represents staff writers from doing certain things such as touching computers in the building or covering stories within city limits. There is never any assurance of steady work, and they can never be sure that their publishers will stand up for them in legal proceedings. Technically, a Freelancer can turn down work. Realistically, he can seldom afford to do so. Why would anybody want to freelance? Because writers have to write and, until the Internet and corporate media killed them, newspapers were the most thrilling, historic, and romantic places to practice the profession of journalism.

Having worked as a television, radio, and newspaper journalist, I prefer newspapers.[2] I was raised on newspapers and the people who wrote them. I was fascinated by Ben Hecht's colorfully embroidered memoir, *A Child of the Century*. I loved the movies, *The Front Page* and *His Girl Friday*. I took print shop every semester in high school. I knew what a byline was long before I earned one, and when I became a movie press agent (sic) after getting out of college, I haunted newspaper offices and drank in newspaper bars and dreamed of crossing the line to become one of them. When I finally did, having given up publicity, the newspapers in the city of Boston, where I lived, were seldom hiring staff, only Freelancers.

---

1. I'm capitalizing *freelancer* because it's the only respect Freelancers get.

2. A fellow journalist (Ron Gollobin) once described the essential difference between a TV news reporter and a newspaper reporter: "When a newspaper reporter gets his story, he goes back to the paper and writes it. The story then goes to the editor, then to rewrite, then to the typesetter, then to the proofreader, then to layout. When a TV reporter comes in from the field, he hands the tape to someone else and goes into hair and makeup."

My editor called. That, in itself, was unusual. According to union rules, he couldn't assign anything to a Freelancer. But like orthodox Jews on the Sabbath, he could drop hints until I caught on.

"You get to spend the summer at Newport at the height of the season," he said. "For free! And you get to mix with movie folks who actually want you on the set and won't have their bodyguards chase you off!"

"Who's landed this plum assignment" I asked?" (Wink wink.)

"Nobody. Yet." (Wink wink.)

"Does it pay the usual fee?"

"For Newport during the season? You—er, whoever writes it—should pay *us*."

"Would the paper pay for the writer's rental car and motel room?"

"Are you out of your mind? I mean, is the eventual writer out of his mind?"

"For once, no. Come on, movie sets are the most boring places in the world. If I go there for six weeks, I won't be able to write movie reviews, business reports, or anything else. Pay me enough to at least break even, and I'd love to do it."

We had a deal. "Anyway," said my editor said, "over the course of six weeks *something* interesting has to happen. Your job is to make sure it sounds like it's happening every day."

Six weeks of assured work was better than six weeks of *looking* for it. A summer in temperate Newport would absolutely be better than steamy Boston. Plus all those movie stars and parties and free drinks.

What I did not realize was that I would get to enjoy none of that.

True, Newport is a lovely town, or so they say. I saw little of it. I spent my time commuting between the locations, my hotel room, and the highway back to Boston, with scant time to sightsee or hang out with cast and crew after hours.

Typically for a location shoot, the movie stars were either acting, rehearsing, studying lines or, at night, resting up. Unfortunately, I could observe none of these activities because I was either writing my own stories or driving the forty miles from Newport to Boston to file them in person at the paper. Because I was not allowed to use the typewriters or computers in the building, I had to drop off my copy in person or find a nighttime editorial staffer to take my dictation over the phone. Sometimes I would even slide past Don, the desk guard, saying I was just stopping in to say hello to someone in the City Room, hiding my manuscript behind me. I'm pretty sure he knew what I was doing. After the first week, these contortions grew tiresome, so someone in editorial had the idea of letting me use one of the paper's two laptop computers. This was not necessarily an improvement. In that nascent Internet era, the only way to uplink to the paper's mainframe computer involved burping the signal from a primitive MODEM through a special set of earphones that cupped onto the telephone handle. It seldom worked; it was easier to drive the forty miles.

On the other hand, I did discover this really great clam shack on the road between Newport and Boston.

I also discovered Ernie Anderson. A former advertising account supervisor, Ernie turned his devotion to Jazz into a lifelong crusade to, as he put it, bring Jazz "out of the saloons and onto the concert stage." That is exactly what he did in 1939 by getting together a group of musicians, including Eddie Condon and Bobby Hackett, and booking them into Carnegie Hall. It was the first time blue notes made the walls of that august venue sigh. Ernie later promoted seven world tours with his long time friend and associate, Louis Armstrong.

Ernie was from the old school, meaning that his handshake was his bond. He was the kind of gentleman they do not make any more, at least not in Hollywood. Today it is corporate and passionless, and publicists know that if this film fails, another one will come along. Because they have the account, and since nobody really know what works, who can blame anybody if it doesn't? Ernie was also only the second person who ever got me to drink Irish whiskey.

As you will read, *Mr. North* turned into a difficult shoot, particularly for Huston's son Danny and daughter Anjelica, both of whom were gracious past expectation during a time that must have been, for them, beyond endurance. Grateful acknowledgement is given to them and to *The Boston Herald*; its publisher Patrick Purcell; city editor Tom Berube; arts editor Bill Weber; assistant arts editor Terry Byrne; editorial assistant Julie Romandetta; executive secretary Phyllis Glidden; librarian John Cronin; and archivist Martha Reagan. Thanks also to the entire cast and crew of *Mr. North*, particularly Karen Golden, David Chapman, Janet Roach, Kal Roberts, and Anthony Edwards.

Thanks, too, to my agent Agnes Birnbaum of Bleecker Street Associates, Inc., Marlene Mattaschiam of The Publicists Guild, Stan Levin, and Mike and Debbi Klein, all of whom had a hand in pulling this project out of the fire at one time or another. My gratitude is also extended to Eddie Brandt's Saturday Matinee and especially to Ben Ohmart and all the folks at BearManor Media.

Finally, undying thanks and love to the Lahmani family—Ami, Ivanna, Adam, and Joseph-Benjamin (JB)—for giving me a reason to keep writing, and sometimes to hide in my office so I can do it.

This book is just one snapshot of a man who led a remarkable life on and off the screen. For a full, rich portrait of John Huston, the Author recommends *The Hustons* by Laurence Grobel (New York: Charles Scriber's Sons, 1988) and Huston's memoir, *An Open Book* (New York: Alfred A. Knopf, 1980). His papers at the Margaret Herrick Library of the Academy of Motion Picture Arts and Sciences are also revealing, and the library itself is a life-saving resource for both film scholars and film fans.

The motion picture *Mr. North* was produced by Heritage Entertainment, Inc. and released in America by The Samuel Goldwyn Company, which transferred the rights to Orion Pictures, and thereafter to MGM/UA. International distribution was through Columbia Pictures. The home video edition from Samuel Goldwyn Home Entertainment was distributed by Virgin Vision, then MGM/UA Home Video. Screenplay extracts are ©1987 Heritage Entertainment, Inc.

Reporters are not welcome on movie sets. Truth be told, I thought that the *Mr. North* company were nuts to have allowed me on theirs. The lessons could not have been lost on them of what Julie Salomon wrote in *The Devil's Candy* about Brian De Palma making *The Bonfire of the Vanities*; what Stephan Farber and Marc Green uncovered in *Outrageous Conduct* about the deaths on *The Twilight Zone: The Movie*; or, closer to home, what Lillian Ross wrote about John Huston during *The Red Badge of Courage* in her seminal 1952 behind-the-scenes book *Picture*. I suspect everyone put up with me for the sake of Danny Huston.

Technically, *Mr. North* was John Huston's last film. Although he didn't direct it, it certainly bears his stamp. His official last film, of course, was *The Dead*, which was released to beatific reviews at the end of 1987. I wrote about *The Dead* in my 2013 BearManor book, *Final Cuts: The Last Films of 50 Great Directors*. But it is my belief that, although *The Dead* got the bulk of the attention, *Mr. North* is the film that allowed John Huston to finally settle affairs with his family, his art, and himself.

– Nat Segaloff
Los Angeles, California

1

Newport

Newport, Rhode Island became the playground of the American aristocracy for a number of reasons. An insulating two hundred miles from New York City, Newport can be reached both by car and boat. More likely though, it was reached by limousine and yacht, which were the favored personal conveyances of the eastern tycoons who were the chief beneficiaries of the Gilded Age. Like today's pirates who build McMansions (only not as tacky) and destroy working-class communities through gentrification, these robber barons commissioned the country's greatest architects and the world's finest craftsmen to build vast homes which they christened with mystical names:

Cottage: The Breakers
Owner: Cornelius Vanderbilt
Fortune: steamships and railroads

Cottage: Chateau-Sur-Mer
Owner: William Shepard Wetmore
Fortune: China trade

Cottage: Rosecliff
Owner: Hermann Oerlichs
Fortune: Comstock Lode

Cottage: The Elms
Owner: Edward Julius Berwind
Fortune: Pennsylvania coal

Cottage: Kingscote
Owner: George Noble Jones
Fortune: southern planter

Cottage: Hunter House
Owner: Jonathon Nichols, Jr.
Fortune: mercantile

Cottage: Isaac Bell House
Owner: Isaac Bell
Fortune: cotton

Cottage: Marble House
Owner: William K. Vanderbilt
Fortune: steamships and railroads

These denizens of the Gilded Age sought respite from the pressures of their daily tasks—tasks that included, not infrequently, the buying and selling of economies—with summer vacations. Life was good for them. They acquired vast land from the U.S. Government in exchange for building the railroads; their mercantile trade was protected by the Navy; their foreign plantations were safeguarded by the Army; their factories were staffed by men, women, and children as yet unrecognized by labor unions and kept in line by Pinkerton thugs; taxes did not exist; and the marketplace was unregulated. Naturally, by the time summer crawled into New York City, they were ready to escape to more relaxing climes. Newport Harbor and Narragansett Bay in Rhode Island offered generous mooring for their vessels, and America gave them unfettered freedom to pursue their dreams.

Founded in 1639 as a settlement for refugees fleeing religious intolerance, the colony flourished in the early 1800s by serving as a port of the notorious "Triangle Trade" of slavery. Its position as a shipbuilding town gave its citizens the money to erect wooden houses, many of which still stand and are among the oldest surviving structures in America.

By the 1850s, however, it was not shipbuilding but mansion building that brought prosperity to Newport. So extensive was the construction, and so well-heeled the clientele, that Newport became, until as late as 1900, Rhode Island's *de facto* state capitol. It was only at the turn of the century that the General Assembly voted to remain in Providence and not rotate with Newport.

The men behind the mansions were not fazed by such local decrees. They were, after all, the people who, more palpably than governments, made America run.

They wanted their playground.

It would have been nothing to loot the world for its culture, if not its artifacts, but, with few exceptions, the millionaires remained atypically conservative in erecting their palaces. To Newport in the mid-nineteenth century were brought craftsmen in marble, glass, architecture, fabric, and cabinet making, plus any and all custom materials they might need in applying their trade. Along Newport's "Millionaires' Row" (Bellevue Avenue) were erected dozens of estates, each more opulent than the last. Cooled by Newport's gentle ocean breezes, they were occupied barely three months a year by the owners who insisted on calling them, with sardonic understatement, "cottages."

The typical "cottage" (whose owner might blanch to hear it called "typical") might contain thirty fully decorated rooms, have the finest tapestry on its walls, polished marble stones, mirrors from floor to twenty-foot ceiling, and graced with the kind of ornate filigree that one would expect around greeting cards, not doorways. Staircases were constructed to allow ladies their grand entrances. Ballrooms fed into meticulously tended gardens and topiaries, and from there spread onto lawns and playing fields overlooking the water. Spewing fountains challenged the surf for attention and generally won; the white-skinned ladies of the age had no need for Newport's sunny beaches, which were left for the townspeople to enjoy.

Indeed, the last place that polite society would find itself was the beaches. Who had the time? A typical socialite's daily schedule—remember that this was during the Gilded Age when *summer* was a verb—began when he or she arose, usually at the crack of noon. After ablutions, one proceeded to the breakfast room where the meal was waiting on the sideboard with polished silver service. Newspapers would be read, and details of the previous night's party would be shared. Afternoons were free and were often taken with visits to neighbors on their established "at home" days when the lady of the cottage received guests, followed by tea and a nap, all in preparation for the coming evening's revelry.

A change into formal clothes, never before six, and never the same gown, followed, and the carriage would draw to the front of the cottage in time to collect its charges for dinner at eight in another socialite's formal dining room. Dancing in the ballroom followed till the wee hours, and one was back in bed by four or five A.M. It all happened again the next day, every day, until September (this was well before there was a Labor Day).

There were, of course, exceptions to these rites, but they were no less romantic. The regatta or steeplechase were respected seasonal rituals that drew fashionable crowds to the country clubs and then into the pages of the society column of Newport's *Mercury*, a publication begun in the 1700s by James Franklin, Benjamin's brother. Fashion dictated fads and games specific to Newport: polo and tennis were developed here, the Tennis Hall of Fame is located on Bellevue just down from Millionaires' Row, and soon after became part of the national fabric. A fabric sporting gold brocade, to be sure.

No one will ever know how much it all cost. There were no taxes and few records. The estates along Bellevue, down equally handsome Ocean Drive, and the sights of Cliff Walk could not be repeated today, and were monumental accomplishments even then. The artisans summoned to America to wield their chisels and palettes for the mansions brought with them, in turn, their families, their apprentices, and their apprentices' families. Men and women who were in service, some of them not much further removed from the Ould Sod than their employers, took up residence either in the attics of the mansions or in the growing number of boarding houses that clustered in the adjacent community. In effect, a separate town grew up around a playground: there were the rich people, and there were those who waited on them. When the Navy built its War College in Newport in the 1880s, the resort community grew even larger.

For the most part, one side did not bother the other. The rich, after all, were only in town three or four months of the year; the rest of the time, Newport was for the regular folks. That kind of tension is still evident today. Although the population is barely 30,000, the town remains divided into two distinct social sets. The year-rounders, by and large, have moved from fishing and manufacturing to a service economy. Gone are the rich robber barons and their libertine parties of the Jazz Age, although there remains a steady flow of their scions and pretenders to the clubs, bars, and resorts that turned Newport's dock district into a Prep School honky-tonk.

Newport in the season is not an effusive town, but it is a polite one. This is remarkable, considering that its summer streets are almost constantly congested with tourists en route to gawk at the mansions which, following the Great Depression, fell into monstrous disrepair and only recently were favored with restoration, and, of course, to wager on Jai-Alai.

On those momentous occasions when the America's Cup competition brings in the yachting set, Newport's hoteliers and restaurateurs happily gouge them on hotel and food prices, and the locals take private glee in giving out wrong driving directions. The posted speed limit in Newport and neighboring Middletown is 20 miles per hour, and it is rigidly observed by every blue-haired resident in his or her eight-cylinder land yacht that meanders through town. On hot days it is common to encounter gridlock by tourists wandering in and out of antique shops and art galleries. The money flows, not from the pampered rich, this time, but from person to person, each wanting a souvenir of a time that only lives in diaries and picture books.

It was to this comfortable resort community that didn't need them or want them that the *Mr. North* company, which included some of the greatest past and future screen stars, came to make their movie.

2

Budget Motor Inn

Not everything in Newport is a mansion. Before you even get there, you hit Middletown.

Despite its name, Middletown, Rhode Island is not really in the middle of anything, except, perhaps, the exit onto Route 114 off the Interstate from Fall River. After a few miles, 114 changes its name to West Main Road, and about half a mile past the shopping mall, on the left, is the Budget Motor Inn; street number 1185, to be exact. These days it's part of the Travelodge chain, but in 1987 it was where the Los Angeles crew and some of the actors were billeted during the six-week shoot. Their room and board were paid by the production company. Locally hired crew, small part players, and extras would commute from their nearby homes.

And now a few words about film crews on location.

Motels and film crews have a testy relationship. The days are long gone when hostelries posted signs saying "No dogs or actors allowed." And thanks to housing laws, motels have to accept pretty much anybody who can pay for a room without destroying it. Depending on the motel, customers know exactly the bang they are getting for the buck. What is important to location film crews, who may stay in the same hotel for weeks or months, are privacy and security, and as long as the sheets and towels are changed daily, all's right with the world.[1] Crews leave early in the day and arrive late at night. They need in-room refrigerators and a wake-up system that works.

Film crews on location can also be cantankerous. After hours, they will drink at the drop of a bottle opener, romance the locals at the drop

---

1. The old joke goes, "They change the sheets every day—between the rooms."

of a room key, and give anything within eyesight a nickname, generally derogatory. For example, portable lavatories are called the "honey wagon" for reasons that have nothing to do with the smell of honey. The catering had better be good or it is sure to earn the scatological seal of disapproval. A tough production manager will be lucky to last a week without being discussed in anatomical terms. Finally, the lodging is certain to take on its own nickname before the first miniature bar of soap has been unwrapped.

The Budget Motor Inn was quickly called by her loving guests, speaking with a French accent, the "Boo-jay Rez-i-dawnce."

The word *motel* is a portmanteau of *motor* and *hotel*. Most of them seem to be orange. Maybe it was a law when they were built, usually in the 1950s, when they were putting up the interstate highway system. As generic as they are on the outside, they can be warm and homey on the inside depending on who runs them. The Budget could boast of Sylvia the Bookkeeper. Besides the books, Sylvia was also in charge of the front desk during the day and managed to keep her aplomb while a pageant of Hollywood types waltzed in and out of the cabin that doubled as her office.

The Budget is a two-story structure that zigzags like a carpenter's folding ruler across a paved blacktop. In 1987, at least, it had no pool, no ice machine, only one shade tree, no room service, no bar, no restaurant, and maybe a vending machine. The only repast within walking or crawling distance was a Ponderosa Steak House, which was conveniently open for breakfast, but the health-conscious visiting Californians soon started foraging on their own. Some went so far as to sublet local apartments, figuring to pool their per diems, or daily cash expenses, and send their paychecks home intact. Even at the height of the vacation season, two people could afford a $1200/month apartment and make out, if not like robber barons, then at least like roommates. Given the 12-hour days and six-day weeks that union crews work on location, a room, whether in a motel or an apartment, is seldom used for anything beyond sleeping and showering. For anything else, you go to her place.

Some of the actors demanded better, and got it. It was not only their salaries that allowed them to rent summer homes near the seashore, but a provision of their Screen Actors Guild contracts that provided them with first-class hotels or separate lodging. As often as not, this was as much for security as status; if word got out that Anthony Edwards, then the co-star of the theatrical smash hit *Top Gun*, and, later, of television's popular *E.R.*, was accessible, he would have been swamped by fans. So Tony rented a house on less-than-elegant-sounding Goat Isle, clear across town. Others, such as Robert Mitchum, stayed at classier hotels nearer the center of town and its taverns. Anjelica Huston found a restored carriage house and, when space opened up in her building, Harry Dean Stanton moved into another unit. Lauren Bacall favored a secluded house among the Newport royalty on Bellevue, and the other major players could be found at the local Sheraton. A few, such as Chris Lawford and Richard Woods, commuted from their homes as their shooting schedule required: Lawford from Boston and Woods from New York.

Some, like the eccentric sprite Tammy Grimes, chose to dwell in the Budget. After barely a week's time, she had decked out her second-story room with antiques, painting supplies, extra furniture and an ever-expanding rock collection.

As the primary crew hang-out, the Budget morphed into a college dormitory. Sound recordists Bill Randall and his son Bill, Jr. set up a charcoal grill and held nightly cookouts. Many rented room refrigerators and stockpiled yogurt and cold cuts. Others, like press-agent-not-publicist Ernie Anderson kept to his daytime diet of milk and Graham crackers, and saved his nighttime tastes for Newport's fine restaurants. The producers, Arthur "Skip" Steloff and Steven Haft, stayed in the Budget to keep watch over their production. So did the director, Danny Huston.

As the man in charge of the film, Danny Huston, age 25 and John's younger son, could have lived anywhere. As it was, he spent more time at the old Newport YMCA where the production stored many of its costumes and props, and where editor Roberto Silvi had set up his editing console in a secluded corner. But it was generally agreed that Danny had been urged to live among his crew by his father, a past master at compensating for low budgets by inspiring high morale among those who worked for him.

John Huston himself, however, would have none of that plebian nonsense; he had long since earned better. Besides, as executive producer, actor, co-screenwriter, and Legend, he could live wherever he damn well pleased and could convince the producers to pay for. During the making of *Mr. North*, his home was on Tuckerman Road, a carefully secluded portion of Newport overlooking rocky cliffs which, despite their rustic beauty, would become the last sights he saw on earth. The house was named "Sea Meadow," and Huston moved in after the weekend of July 4, 1987. He and his companion, Maricela Hernandez, set up house, he to polish the screenplay with Janet Roach, and Maricela to look after his wellbeing. The house was notable for its nearly flat interior. Aside from three steps into the sunken living room, the rest of the residence, from its front door to its hallway and bedrooms, demanded no climbing. This layout was crucial to Huston's health, for the then 80-year-old lion was in the advanced stages of emphysema and found it necessary to traverse his world in a wheelchair.

Unable to benefit even from Newport's relatively unpolluted air, Huston endured his progressive illness by means of oxygen fed to him from a tank in the center of the house, through a tangle of clear plastic tubing that ran up his back, around his ears, and under his nose. He could withstand being off the machine for up to twenty minutes at a time, long enough to perform as an actor in his scenes, but then had to get back on again. The oxygen tank, the location of the house, and the physical distance between him and the film were to become an issue as filming wore on.

With cast and crew thus scattered across Middletown and Newport, the production office coordinated the disparate participants. Ann Shaw was the married daughter of Tommy Shaw, Huston's longtime production manager and a pit bull of a man, and she ran the office from a first-floor suite at the Budget Motor Inn. A friendly woman who could turn fiercely protective if the situation required it, Ann handled the countless requests for rides, rooms, and other details. From her, came shipping instructions, scheduling, and the myriad tiny tasks that combine to make a film run efficiently. She was also the one who got stuck telling tourists who stumbled into her office instead of Sylvia's cabin looking for vacancies that the motel's rental office was back up the road and that they had passed it. In the production office were several phones, always busy; an exhausted photocopy machine; a bulletin board on which messages could be posted; and the constantly updated records of the ongoing shoot. Next door was a separate accounting office whose job was to process paychecks, especially for extras called upon to lend their presence, but not their personality, to crowd scenes.

A film is a short-term business enterprise created to produce a product that lives beyond the lifetime of those who work on it. Every movie has to balance complex financial and legal needs as well as creative and intellectual property issues. The animal has to eat, and breathe, and sleep, and poop, and it all takes place, so to speak, in the production office.

But when John Huston moved into the house on Tuckerman at the beginning of July, those kind of details weren't his concern. He and Danny had to bring the performances together, introduce the actors to their characters, and forge an ensemble. They achieved this with read-throughs and rehearsals held around the dinner table and on the back lawn. Normally, money-conscious producers do not want to pay actors until they are needed in front of the cameras. They hate to spring for rehearsals. But this was different. Huston had the power to demand it. Even if he didn't, what actor would want to miss working with him? By Sunday, July 26, the players were beginning to come together, and plans were made to start shooting on Monday the 27th. It was a sleepy Sunday in Newport, the last day to relax before a six-week ordeal. Danny went to work finalizing the script, but John, who was to act the role of crusty old John McHenry Bosworth on Tuesday morning, decided to take the rest of the day off. That afternoon he invited some friends over to do what he liked doing best, maybe even better than picture making, if the two interests could ever be considered separate: gambling.

3

John Huston

I did not know John Huston; I still don't. I am not sure it was possible to know him, at least, not all of him, he had so many facets. True, I conducted his last interview, but that's not saying much because it wasn't much of an interview. It was less an interview than sharing a few moments, complementing him on his work—can you imagine a more obvious task?—and letting him relax instead of speak. No, I was not simply showing consideration to a tired, ill man; not really. I was being tactful. Sometimes good interviews start when you pretend you don't want one. This never did.

Mostly, I just wanted to see if I could get him to call me "kid."

"Kid" was what he called people he worked with in a familiar, almost paternal way. Though perhaps it spared him the effort of remembering names. A man who could make himself at home anywhere in the world shouldn't be expected to know everyone personally. Even though I hadn't worked with him, it was still a dream.

We had actually seen each other before, in New York City, in 1980, in the Plaza Hotel elevator, of all places. He was in Manhattan hawking his autobiography *An Open Book*, and I was attending a press junket for a movie whose title now escapes me. Naturally, I could name dozens of Huston's films, and had even reviewed a couple of his later ones when I was on Boston's CBS radio station, WEEI-FM. I was aware of their diversity, not only of style, but of competence. It was baffling. How could the director of *The Maltese Falcon*, a seminal mystery, also make the disjointed mystery *The Mackintosh Man*? How could the leaden *Annie* come from the same man who had made *The Treasure of the Sierra Madre*? How could the wonderfully goofy *Beat the Devil*, the brutal *The Asphalt Jungle* and the sublime *The African Queen* share a filmography with *The Kremlin Letter* and *The Bible*?

Danny Huston explained this phenomenon to me by relating how producer interference can be so destructive, quoting his father and imitating his well-known voice: "They want us to make baaaaad pictures? Very well, we can make them baaaaad. They'll cost more, but they will be baaaaad."

As a result, I didn't know where to start, and the elevator was rapidly descending. There was the towering Huston, dressed in a white plantation suit and flowered necktie, leaning jauntily on his walking stick while watching the floor numbers. There was I doing none of the above. All I could do was introduce myself as a movie critic and say I was here for a publicity junket and that I appreciated his work.

"That's grand," he smiled, then added, "I do wish you'd say something about my book." Within his soft voice was both a request and a command.

"Of course I will," I said. "Are you getting set to make another film?"

"Well, we're still trying to get Malcolm Lowry's *Under the Volcano* financed. It's always difficult finding money for something that's about people instead of automobiles."

"I want to thank you for *The Man Who Would Be King*," I offered. "It's only one of the greatest adventure films ever made."

Huston smiled tightly. "You know, I first tried to make that with Bogey and Clark Gable, but the money never came together. But I think Michael and Sean did a splendid job." Michael Caine and Sean Connery. The man dropped names other people couldn't even lift. "Well," he said, stepping off, "here's the lobby." I hadn't even heard the elevator bell chime, and my audience was over.

Our paths never crossed for an actual on-the-record talk; Freelancers have little pull to land prestigious interviews. When you don't write for the *Times*, people don't bend their schedules to fit yours.

The Newport encounter wasn't an interview; it was a poker game. Ernie Anderson and I found the house and pulled into the gravel driveway. Janet Roach, with whom he had written *Prizzi's Honor* and shared an Academy Award® nomination, greeted us and told Maricela, who was preparing lunch, that we had arrived. We waited in the vestibule while Ernie discretely asked Janet about Huston's health, which also, of course, was an inquiry about the health of the production. The two men had worked together for decades, and the relationship had broadened far beyond that of director and press agent, even if they did manage to see each other only during films or when they happened to be in the same town between films. Anderson had become the keeper of the Huston legend, a mission that included not only brokering press time with the man but maintaining a family chronicle.[1]

It was immediately apparent that the two friends had not seen each other for months. The unflappable Anderson's face betrayed shock when he saw Huston. Gaunt, wearing loose house clothes that draped from his shoulders, his unshaven face a pallid grey and his once-sparkling eyes sunk into grey-rimmed sockets, Huston smiled from the oval dining room table where the poker table was set up. He sat in a wheelchair. The life-giving oxygen tubes hung around his neck and, despite their near-weightlessness, seemed to pull him down. An aluminum walker stood against the wall.

His breathing was heavy, but that wonderful, melodious voice was intact, even if it could only speak a few words before needing air.

"How good to see you again, Ernie," he said. "Please, please come in. Come on over here where I can see you." Huston smiled that courtly, closed-mouth smile for which he was famous—the one that could melt a resistant actor into submission, or wordlessly inform a doubting studio executive just who the director was.

Playing poker at the broad, oval living room table were: actor Harry Dean Stanton, co-producer Steven Haft, Michael Fitzgerald who was here as a visitor but was producer of Huston's *Wise Blood* and, yes, *Under the Volcano*, which they finished in 1984, film editor Roberto Silvi (*The Dead*) and, of course, the man himself.

Even ravaged by age and disease, Huston sat tall in his chair. The man whose entire life was a poker game had no trouble playing it with cards. Specifically, it was a game of "Hold 'em" that Stanton had just dealt.

"You look fine, Ernie," Huston pronounced.

"So do you, John," Ernie lied.

I was introduced, and Huston was told that I would be writing daily stories about the production.

Huston carefully placed his cards face down in front of him and extended his hand. "That's fine," he said, "that's fine." His grip was strong, assured. No wonder he had chased Death away so often.

"I hope we'll have the time to talk," I said as another cough climbed

---

1. My copy of which I donated to the Margaret Herrick Library of the Academy of Motion Picture Arts and Sciences.

up Huston's chest. He returned to his game and introductions with the other players were concluded. Michael Fitzgerald and I had met before and had friends in common, which he remembered.

Poker is not a spectator sport. Huston studied his cards as if he wished he could rewrite his hand, but his concentration seemed tenuous. Without making it obvious, Stanton and Fitzgerald found ways to remind him when it was his bet and what the last raise had been.

In his prime, Huston was known as a gambler—thousands at a time when he had it, and frequently when he didn't—and, in this heady crowd, the fives and tens piled in the center of the table were daunting.

"Bet's to you," Steve Haft reminded Huston, who contemplated a raise.

"Okay," he said. "I'll go ten."

Stanton was next. "Ten?" he confirmed. "Well, okay, count me in a dime." He later claimed he lost $300 that day.

After another round in which Huston dealt the cards with practiced ease, Ernie rose to leave.

"You're staying for lunch?" the all-seeing Janet Roach asked from the next room.

"No," Ernie begged off. "We have to do some work. Just came by to say hello."

"Goodbye, Ernie," Huston said as everybody else nodded or mumbled similar valedictions. "Good to see you again, Ernie," Huston repeated. "You're looking well."

Later, in the car, Ernie was angry.

"Huston looks just terrible," he said. "He gets worse if he's not working on something. That's why it's best that he's kept busy. If they don't keep him busy…" He paused. "It isn't good. You saw how he looked."

I did. I thought about the jaunty Huston in his white suit strutting through the Plaza lobby seven years earlier and compared it with the wizened old man sitting in a wheelchair deciding whether to raise a ten dollar bet.

John Huston once said of his life, in summary, "It certainly has been an occasion." Driving into the hot afternoon that Sunday in July, I knew which occasion I wanted to remember.

4

A Glorious Adventure

Before he started, John Huston issued a statement about Newport and the film he was there to make:

> For half a century I've been admiring the writings of Thornton Wilder. Now it's brought us here to Newport and I find I've fallen in love with the place. We're all quite excited—my daughter, my son, our whole company. We have the feeling that we're about to embark on a glorious adventure.

It was impossible to tell whether Huston was being prescient, polite, or nostalgic in saying this in the way he said it. His comments were the kind of sunny, perfunctory words a celebrity or diplomat might offer to inquiring reporters covering the embarkation of an ocean liner. It was a kind of elegant, albeit meaningless, "Have a nice day." Yet Huston was not mimicking that genteel era, he was a remnant of it, and he certainly meant what he said. This was, after all, the man who lived the word *adventure*: braving the Congo with *The African Queen*, exploring Morocco with *The Man Who Would Be King*, taming Mexico for *The Treasure of the Sierra Madre*, and fighting the likes of Jack Warner, Louis B. Mayer, Harry Cohn, and Darryl F. Zanuck in Hollywood.

Huston's gracious manner was his nod to the style of the project itself. Thornton Wilder wrote *Theophilus North* at the end of his life. It was published in 1973; Wilder died two years later. There is speculation that he was not terribly satisfied with the way the book had turned out. Wilder, a triple Pulitzer Prize winner, was known for his tight construction, precise dialogue, and focus of his themes. *Theophilus North* is an amorphous and meandering work, as some of the actors confided after they had slugged through its 374 pages in preparation for their roles. The book reads more like an old man's resolving of his life than a brilliant writer's evocation of an era, as was, for example, Booth Tarkington's *The Magnificent Ambersons*.

Set in Newport in 1926 on the eve of the Great Depression, the novel has much on its mind. Yale graduate Theophilus North, played in the film by Anthony Edwards, quits his job tutoring a gaggle of rich brats and peddles his talents to a more appreciative clientele. Literally pedaling, he rides his bicycle to Newport, Rhode Island where he finds a part-time job reading scripture to the feisty millionaire John McHenry Bosworth. Bosworth, of course, has no need of hearing scripture; it is merely the plan of his conniving daughter, Sara Baily-Lewis, played by Tammy Grimes, to keep him housebound. Sara pretends to enrich her father's life while, in actuality, she is embarrassed by his incontinence and has designs on his estate. She is joined in her scheme by Dr. Angus McPherson, played by David Warner, the local society physician whose patients never seem to recover. Bosworth's granddaughter, Persis Tennyson, played by Anjelica Huston, is a young widow whose willowy manner suggests that she knows nothing of this conspiracy of wills, not to mention Wills, but nevertheless has her doubts. She also comes to set her eye on Theophilus.

There are more complications. No sooner does word get around that the latest rage in Newport is for beneficiaries to knock off their not-quite-dead-yet benefactors, it is also learned that the people who keep this from happening are the servants. Newport's working class, headed by butler Henry Simmons, played by Harry Dean Stanton, has become the town's unofficial police force. Many of them dwell in a boarding house run by Mrs. Amelia Cranston, played by Lauren Bacall, a retired servant who saved her money and invested it in real estate. North quickly discovers that the serving class has a social structure as intricate as that of the blue-bloods.

Theophilus North, or "Mr. North," as he is called, becomes the link between these two diverse worlds. Friendly with the servants but not permitted to live among them (because nobody who uses the front door of the cottages may room with those who must use the rear entrance), he takes up residence at the local YMCA. That segregation, however, does not keep him from becoming involved with the lives of all the people he meets, sometimes in unusual ways. His short-lived romance with servant

Sarah Boffin, played by Virginia Madsen, gives her the confidence to seek a future elsewhere, and, in fact, she finds a husband in Michael P. Ennis, played by Christopher Lawford. With Elspeth Skeel, played by Mary Stuart Masterson, his unusual ability to build up a static electric charge seems to cure the girl's migraine headaches, causing Dr. McPherson to haul him into court for practicing medicine without a license. That is when Mr. and Mrs. Skeel, played by Mark Metcalf and Katharine Houghton, lend their support in what becomes a groundswell of affection for North from the entire town, which thereby comes to understand the meaning of optimism.

Wilder was not enough of an optimist himself, however, and definitely not enough of a Marxist, to suggest that this groundswell might result in the unity of the classes. He just wanted to show that one man can make a difference if other men and women are open to change.

The real trick in getting *Mr. North* to the screen was condensing Wilder's spongy book into a filmable screenplay of ninety-six pages. To do so, writers Huston and Roach tried to distill the essence of *Theophilus North* while keeping it from being a soap opera like *Upstairs, Downstairs*, whose success on public television limited any further attempt at period domestic drama. The original script had been written by James Costigan,[1] a veteran of such Golden Age television anthologies as *Studio One, United States Steel Hour*, and *G.E. Theatre* where he specialized in adaptations of *Wuthering Heights, A Doll's House, The Turn of the Screw*, etc. Costigan broke the book's spine, as they say in screenwriting parlance, but it took Huston and Roach to refine the characters enough to make the project appealing to bankable actors.

Three problems immediately complicated *Mr. North*, which is what the producers believed would be a more commercial title than one containing the word *Theophilus*. The first, and this became less of a problem as history moved along, was that, when the film was being shot in the summer of 1987, there was another Mr. North, Marine Lieutenant Colonel Oliver North, whose name confused the issue.[2] That passed.

The second was trickier. In a film with so many characters and so little screen time to establish them, executive producer Huston called upon his

---

1. Costigan died in 2007 at age 81. *Mr. North* was his final credit.

2. Familiar then, nostalgic now. Lt. Col. North was tried for his role in the Reagan Administration's illegal sale of military weapons to Iran in order to raise money for their equally illegal support of the Contra army in Nicaragua. The scandal was uncovered in 1986.

friends to help out. Movie stars are recognizable; that is why they're movie stars. Putting a big one in a small role helps the audience know who is who right from the start. Usually, stars of that magnitude don't take small roles, and, if they do, rarely take small salaries. Laurence Olivier, for example, who spent a great deal of his later life playing supporting roles, once said, "I don't mind being thought of as a small-part actor, but after a while they tend to think of you in terms of a small-part actor's *salary*, and that I *do* mind."[3] On the other hand, the person asking them to do the job was Huston, and that is different. Vastly different. They did it for him, as well as for Danny. In a business not known for loyalty, there was a great deal of it going around.

The third problem was, frankly, one of public scholarship. The story was set in the 1920s. It was being made for 1980s audiences. As L. P. Hartley wrote in *The Go-Between*, "The past is a foreign country; they do things differently there." The Jazz Age, despite its reputation for bathtub gin and hot-and-cold running Charlestons, was a more literate, formal era with less slang, or at least a clear demarcation between who used it and who did not. There were manners and conventions that have become foreign to most current moviegoers and, to a large extent, to most modern movie stars. Like Shakespeare, some words just do not seem to fit in some mouths. It became Danny Huston's job to see that they did.

Danny, 25 at the time, is the son of Huston by Zoë Sallis, the woman Huston knew while separated from his fourth wife, dancer Ricki Soma. If it sounds complicated, well, the Hustons are a complicated family. What is not complicated was the degree of John Huston's devotion to his children; it was total. Just as his famous father, Walter Huston, encouraged young John and often lent his acting presence to the lad's films (most notably with an Oscar®-winning performance in *The Treasure of Sierra Madre*), so did John endeavor to see that his children became successful.

His older son, Tony, is a screenwriter, and adapted James Joyce's *The Dead* which John directed before starting *Mr. North*. Anjelica is a star actress, whose Oscar® for *Prizzi's Honor* was assisted by her father, who directed her. Both Tony and Anjelica are his children with Ricki Soma. Alegra, Soma's daughter, whom John embraced as his own, became a successful editor working in London. And Danny, for whom *Mr. North* was his first theatrical feature after directing several television films, later became an acclaimed actor (*Two Jacks, X-Men, The Proposition*).

Naturally, John is a part of it all; in addition to serving as executive producer, a supervisory position negotiated by his agent, Paul Kohner,

---

3. Audio interviews for *Sleuth* (1973, Palomar Pictures International).

and having co-written the screenplay, he was expected to play the role of Bosworth. Thus, as Walter did for John, John planned to do for Danny.

With Anjelica in town and rumored to be seeing Jack Nicholson, Zoë living nearby while Maricela is living with John, and Tony and Alegra planning extended visits, the production has become a family affair. An unusual family, to be sure, but family nonetheless.

It was, indeed, the beginning of a glorious adventure.

5

Rolling

Mr. North began filming on Monday, July 26, 1987 under pressure. Even though it is a labor of love and everybody was working below his normal fee, the company still had to meet deadlines and keep the production within its already tight budget. Part of that burden fell to Tommy Shaw, the production manager. The production manager is a crew boss, a foreman whose responsibility is, ultimately, everything and everyone working on the movie. Having collaborated with Huston for most of his career, Shaw knew what corners could be cut and how to let the director have what he wants. When he started managing Danny's production, Shaw become even more devoted to his job, even fanatical. This triggered grumbling among the crew.

Because *Mr. North* was being produced for an independent company on a modest budget, it was granted certain waivers by the Hollywood unions to reduce its crew size and pay people on a different scale than, say, a major studio show. *Mr. North*'s producers eagerly took advantage of the loopholes in Hollywood's legendarily tight labor agreements.

Although actors, even those who weren't members of the omnipotent Screen Actors Guild (SAG), had to be paid at least union scale, many of the technicians were said to have been able to negotiate separate service contracts, eluding the jurisdiction of the fiercely possessive International Alliance of Theatrical Stage Employees (IATSE, sometimes called just "The IA"). The film further benefited from an atmosphere of uncertainty that smothered Hollywood in the summer of 1987 when the all-powerful Directors Guild of America (DGA) failed to finalize agreements with its signatory producers and a strike loomed if an accord was not reached.

Mindful that, without directors, there would be no work, many members of the industry's craft unions panicked and signed on below their usual quotes. Thus, *Mr. North* became what *Variety* called an "indie prod"—independent production—that fell into one of the cracks in the system. By the time the DGA settled with representatives of Hollywood's producers, (the DGA strike lasted, literally, ten minutes) Huston's crew found themselves saddled with agreements that called for 72-hour, six day weeks without overtime.

In truth, most would probably have taken a pay cut just to work with John Huston. Some had served him before and were looking forward to sharing his indefatigable energy, while others, primarily the younger crew members and a handful of non-union newcomers being Taft-Hartleyed in, anticipated meeting the legend. Huston was not scheduled to work Monday, first day of shooting. What would be shot that day was the beginning of a scene which, by its conclusion, would bring Theophilus North together with John McHenry Bosworth. Bosworth's/Huston's call was for Tuesday.

Even before the first frame was shot, there were cast changes. Burgess Meredith, the diminutive powerhouse who appeared in *Of Mice and Men* and *Day of the Locust*, but is probably best known as Sylvester Stallone's trainer in *Rocky*, was slated to play Judge Cadwalader, the jurist into whose courtroom North is dragged by the shady Dr. McPherson. Although Meredith's scenes would not be filmed for a month, word reached Newport that the actor, in whose house Huston had been living before coming east, was ill and would have to withdraw. There was no word on who would replace him in the small but important role. It required little more than sitting on the bench and looking dispassionate, a cameo that any actor would love to fill.

But that was not Danny Huston's concern on the first day of production. He was working with Anthony Edwards, Tammy Grimes, Virginia Madsen and Richard Woods. The scene marked North's (Edwards') arrival at the Bosworth estate, his grilling by Bosworth's daughter, Mrs. Baily-Lewis (Grimes), his sighting of Persis (Anjelica), and his nearly being tossed out of the house by Bosworth's protective butler, Willis (Woods). As North enters the mansion, he witnesses Mrs. Bailey-Lewis berating her servant, Sarah Boffin, who also goes by the name Sally, (Madsen) for cheekiness.

"This does not concern any of you!" Bailey-Lewis informs the other servants, looking at Sarah, who is dusting under the heavy foyer table.

"You too, Dora. Get to your chores."

"Yes, mum," Sarah says, "Only it's not Dora, mum. It's Sarah, same as you."

Mrs. Baily-Lewis recoils at her servant's presumption. "*Same as me?* Impudent child! You are *not* the same as me, and don't you ever forget it. Try to rise above your station in this house, missy, and you'll find yourself back on the Ould Sod emptying chamber pots and doing twice the work for a quarter of the money we pay you!"

Sarah flees the room and Mrs. Bailey-Lewis turns her chilly smile toward the newcomer: "This way, Mr. North," she beams.

There was nothing terribly complicated about the scene, which was purposely scheduled on the first day of production so that cast, crew and director could learn each other's rhythms. In addition to their lines, they also had to remember to treat their ornate surroundings with respect. The location was the Chateau-Sur-Mer, a "cottage" that was being used as a set. But by no stretch of the definition could it be called a set; it was more like a museum (it became a National Historic Landmark in 2006) and its furnishings were hardly props, they were priceless antiques. Chairs that were not being used in front of the cameras were pushed back against the walls, well clear of filmmaking equipment and tired rear ends, and sported signs, "Do not touch."

The Chateau-Sur-Mer was built between 1851 and 1852 by William Shepard Wetmore, whose fortune had been made several times over in the China trade. It was outfitted in the style of the Italian Renaissance and French salons and was restored by the Preservation Society of Newport County whose liaison, Paul Miller, was constantly shooing people away from the chotchkes. Practically everything within sight was an antique, and, except for the actors who used them in the course of a scene, nobody was allowed to touch anything that was not brought in specifically for the scene. Even the rugs were rolled back and cordoned off with yellow "danger" tape. Observers felt as though they were visiting a fussy aunt's house. On the other hand, film crews are notoriously Carthaginian when working on locations, and anybody who lives in Los Angeles knows, without thinking twice about it, never to allow a film crew to shoot anywhere they want to keep intact. Miller was followed around by two apprentices clad in denim and spotless Preservation Society tennis shirts. It was their job to move whatever relics needed moving and to guard those that did not. The rental fees paid by the filmmakers for permission to shoot in the house went straight into the Preservation Society's restoration fund.

Until *Mr. North*, the best-known films to use Newport were the stodgy 1974 remake of *The Great Gatsby* and the trashy 1978 melodrama *The Betsy*. Coincidentally, *Mr. North* cinematographer Robin Vidgeon had worked on *Gatsby* as assistant to director of photography Douglas Slocombe in these same locations thirteen years earlier. While Vidgeon aligned a shot for Danny Huston, Paul Miller nervously watched the grips moving the heavy camera between and among the house's priceless fittings. Satisfied that none of the woodwork was being scratched, he returned to his historical concerns.

"Chateau-Sur-Mer is one of the earliest examples of the more formal summer cottages in Newport," he explained. "William Shepard Wetmore was active in social circles and died in 1862, having left the Chateau to his 16-year-old son, George Peabody Wetmore. Young Wetmore traveled and appreciated art, and employed architects and artists to expand the house and inspire the interiors."

Miller allowed that the Hollywood crew was respectful of the premises, but he nevertheless watched them cautiously. "This house is still in restoration," he said, "and we want it better known, so we allow filming. The Preservation Society of Newport County is a non-profit organization. It receives very little state or federal support. Ninety percent of its revenues come from admission fees paid by visitors, and the rest comes from memberships, of which there are several thousand people interested in Newport architecture. It's patron money. And, of course, film rentals like this."

Smiling at mention of a supernatural footnote to the town's history, Miller said that there were no ghosts that haunt the mansions, but averred that memories of past events were very much present. "The most notable party given here was given by William Shepard Wetmore," he recited. "It was a *fete champagne* garden party attended by well over a thousand people, including the President of the United States (Franklin Pierce) with elaborate [dinner] courses. The full estate had several stables and hothouses, and all interiors were filled with the great Newport theme flowers. The American Beauty Rose was created here for the Gilded Age, and also Newport Blue Hydrangeas.

"If one had an aesthetic eye, it was a paradise," Miller continued. "Newport was first painted by the Hudson River School. It was not just a playground or a social capitol, it was a literary center."

Despite the glitter and power of the leading nobs, the lives of the town's average people were never chronicled. "There is very little written on the daily lives in Newport," Miller revealed. "Most of it is centered on the memoirs of the society figures or best-selling novels of the Gilded Age, both historical and fictional. Other than the summer colony, life here is not that well documented. We're now doing a series of oral histories amongst the working class people of the city who were associated with the summer people—tradesmen, servants, gardeners and others who are still alive.

"There's not the class rivalry that used to exist. Most of the cottages today are either multi-family dwellings, museums, dormitories [Salve Regina College is nearby] or condominiums. Most of the grand scale living of this society has vanished or, if it's still present at all, is fairly low key. There's no Old Guard any more; a good many younger families have moved in."

While Miller narrated the changing fortunes of Newport, actors Grimes and Edwards and director Danny Huston ran the dialogue that would lead to the reveal of Bosworth, who would be played by John Huston. Those scenes would be shot the next day, Tuesday.

"As I told you on the telephone," Grimes instructs Edwards in the throaty voice that made her one of the most distinctive actresses of her generation, "I wish you to read to my father. My father is eighty-one years old. He needs the solace of hearing the Good Book."

"I see," says Edwards, not swayed by her regal attitude, especially after witnessing the outburst against Sarah. He realizes, as does she, that Mrs. Bailey-Lewis, despite her airs, is not that far away from the Ould Sod herself.

"Your advertisement said you charge two dollars an hour," she haggles, rejecting his request for $150 and leading to a discussion of how fast he should read, which language to use, and what the whole arrangement should cost.

"You gave me to understand your interest was in speed, not intelligibility," Edwards tells Grimes, calling her on her attitude, "in which case, I'll tell you what else I can do: I am going to read the Sermon on the Mount in exactly four minutes and fifty-one seconds. If I go one second over that mark, I will absolutely and positively knock another five dollars off this already rock bottom price!"

"That's enough of your blasphemy, Mr. North," Grimes exclaims. But Edwards persists.

"Shall we say an even $130, no questions asked?" he says.

"I think you'd better go, Mr. North. Kindly leave this house at once!"

"Cut," said Danny, pleased with the intensity from his actors. The lengthy scene enabled Grimes and Edwards to reach a level of sustained performance and concentration unusual for modern, quickly edited movies, and this seemingly anachronistic, but classical, dialogue gave them satisfaction. The director then called for additional set-ups from several more angles, called "coverage," for editing purposes.

The filming took place in a cramped anteroom, and without the space to allow fluid camera movement or complicated staging, it threatened to look boring on screen. Danny opted for having Grimes and Edwards enter the room, stand briefly in place, then sit on a sofa against the curtained window. This meant that Vidgeon and gaffer (lighting) Ross Maehl had to be alert to changes in sunlight behind the actors and boost it when Nature changed her f-stop. But it was the only way to enliven a scene whose energy comes from verbal jousting, not motion.

Outside Chateau-Sur-Mer, the rest of the team waited. Waiting is the second most frequent activity in movie-making. At any given time on a film set it, it looks as though only half of the people are working, and the rest are standing around. This is true, but unavoidable. When the cameras roll, crew members who were involved in preparing the shot must wait to be summoned back to prep the next one, and then trade places with the acting and shooting half. Since all of the day's scenes took place inside the Chateau, it was impossible, given the cramped quarters, to do anything but leapfrog teams. Those who were not needed inside were held by second assistant director Joe Brooks until the all-clear was issued over his walkie-talkie.

But there was still activity on the edge of the set, in a side room of the Chateau. That was where costume designer Rita Riggs, wardrobe chief Deborah Newhall, and assistants Ann Smith, Marilyn Salvatore, and Karen Gilbert made sure that actors and extras were fitted, matched continuity from scene to scene, and returned their duds when finished. Makeup artists Bob Arrollo, Keis Maes, and Fern Buckner also used this room, along with hairstylists Frida Aradottir and Anthony Cortino.

Waiting in the lounge was Anjelica Huston who dropped by the set to visit, even though she would not be needed in makeup and costume until late in the day; Grimes' earlier reference to her would be paid off by an off screen cutaway. Sitting on a window seat in the darkened room, her face lit softly by sunlight reflected off the Chateau's lawn, she relaxed with a book. She didn't need to watch her half-brother, Danny, at work; it was enough for him just to know that she was there. This was a time to renew friendships with the people she had worked with on *Prizzi's Honor* and *The Dead*.

The first day of shooting sets the tone for every film. Get ahead of schedule, and it suggests a pace that may tire the company before the film is completed; fall behind, and it forms a cloud from which it is not easy to emerge. Wise production managers schedule easy-to-do scenes for Day One, and Tommy Shaw was such a man.

Besides, this film did not have the luxury of languor. It would not do well to be behind when John Huston arrived on the set the next morning. It was what everyone had been waiting for, and why they had come in the first place.

6

Emergency

On Tuesday July 27, instead of going to the set, John Huston went to the hospital. The newspaper read:

> Legendary Hollywood director John Huston was rushed to the hospital yesterday afternoon in what a spokesman called "grave condition."
>
> The 80-year-old Huston was leaving his rented house to drive to a mansion location where he was to begin filming *Mr. North* when he fell ill and was taken by ambulance to Charlton Memorial Hospital in Fall River.
>
> Producer Skip Steloff of Heritage Entertainment was with Huston when he became ill and later told the *Herald*, "He'll be out in less than a week . . . that buffalo is so tough."

Steloff did not know it then, but that was not the truth. Huston would spend the next four weeks at the hospital, an out-of-the-way medical center accustomed to treating the ills of the Newport nobs, and, therefore, more skillful than a big city hospital in deflecting press inquiries. The continuing drama would affect the entire *Mr. North* company.

"I'm a lifelong friend of Mr. Huston," Ernie Anderson assured the stolid hospital worker who blocked his phone call. "All I want to know is what his condition is!" Anderson was held prisoner in his motel room by an unending stream of phone calls, not only from press but from Huston's worldwide *Who's Who* of friends and reporters. The provincial phone service didn't help matters in the pre-cell phone, pre Internet era. And the hospital's over-protective attitude only made things worse. "I'm not authorized to give out that information," the spokeswoman said, admitting nothing beyond Huston's presence at the facility. It took the indefatigable Anderson a quarter of an hour to break through her robotic, disembodied veneer.

"Just tell me his condition," he pleaded. There was a pause as he heard her report. His expression remained stoic. "Would you say his condition is grave?" He covered the mouthpiece and nodded a confirmation, then hung up. His face betrayed his concern. "His condition is grave but there are hopeful signs since he hasn't contracted pneumonia."

As with most chronic diseases, it isn't the disease that does the killing, it's pneumonia or some other opportunistic infection that does in the weakened patent. With emphysema, which systematically reduces the lungs' ability to extract oxygen from the air, and therefore reduces the sufferer's ability to breathe, the jeopardy comes not only from pneumonia but from aspiration. Even a small piece of food that "goes down the wrong tube" can cause choking because the patient does not have enough lung power to cough it out. Eventually there just are not enough functioning cells left and asphyxia occurs. It is a not an easy passing, yet is largely preventable by not smoking.

"You know, he's beat death at least five times," Anderson says, as much for his own reassurance as for information. "The other times, the heart bypass, pneumonia, all that, they figured him for dead, but he beat 'em all. As long as he's working, as long as they keep him busy, he's going to be all right. You'll see."

Expecting her father at the Chateau-Sur-Mer, Anjelica sped from location to the hospital. Danny was obligated to keep the film going, however, and was forced to remain and devise ways of shooting around his father until he was able to come to the set—if he ever could. "I'm confident my father will recover and am hopeful he'll be back on the set before we finish," Danny announced bravely. But the wheels were already turning to recast the part.

Typically, they had been set in motion by Huston himself. "On the way to the hospital, the ailing actor showed his grit by suggesting the name of an international star, even as the ambulance was rushing him there," Anderson stated for the record, then leaned forward with a conspiratorial off-the-record twinkle in his eyes.

"It's Robert Mitchum," he confided. "The producers are on the phone now trying to work it out." That evening, Steven Haft confirmed that there was a search for a replacement, but declined to name names.

Besides, Mitchum was tied up, was he not? Wasn't he in California midway through a complicated shooting schedule for *War and Remembrance*, the follow-up to the popular TV mini-series *The Winds of War*? Certainly, ABC television had no mind to postpone their big show by releasing its star to make an "indie prod" clear across the country.

And there was still hope that Huston would recover in time to shoot his scenes.

"Sunday afternoon, as John was laughing and talking with his guests as he played poker, he seemed to be a paler shadow of his true self and his color was frightening," Anderson recalled for publication. Still, hope is a constant emotion on a Huston set. Wasn't this the man who had just completed an eight-week shoot for *The Dead* from his wheelchair, turning off his oxygen tank during the takes so that the hissing sound wouldn't pick up on the microphones?

"A man who, toward the end of his life, was attached to oxygen tubes and confined mostly to a wheelchair could still be the tallest and most powerful man in a room," Anjelica later recalled.

When they heard the news, the cast and crew remained optimistic.

"For the last week he's been very strong and alert," said Anthony Edwards. "It was a surprise to me. I had no indication. Just three days ago we were having great rehearsals with him. He's been very present in the movie."

Edwards stepped outside the Chateau-Sur-Mer long enough to grab a drink of water and beg away from the gathering press who had started to converge on what was supposed to be a closed set. In the brilliant white suit that becomes his character's trademark, he tried to avoid eye contact with curious hangers-on, and hurried back into the mansion to help Danny continue. It would be tough for both of them, since Danny had to shoot Edwards' close-ups without Edwards having Huston, or anyone, to act against.

When no further word came to the set, conjecture starts that Huston will be replaced as Bosworth, but will return later as Judge Cadwalader, the role that Burgess Meredith had to vacate.

The day went agonizingly slowly, but by 6 PM it was wrapped. Immediately, Danny rushed to join Anjelica at the hospital, a good half hour away from location.

He was carrying with him a secret that the producers had told him only moments earlier, and he was entrusted with the task of informing his ailing father: Robert Mitchum was flying east.

<h1 align="right">7</h1>

Danny Huston

Twenty-five-year-old Danny Huston was alone among others. Although surrounded by his sisters Anjelica and Alegra, brother Tony was working abroad, the crew that was making *Mr. North* had just finished *The Dead* and had been guided into a tight team by the elder Huston. There would be no question, however, that Danny was the director of his film. His word was to be taken as law on the set, yet with such an awesome cast as Lauren Bacall, Harry Dean Stanton, Tammy Grimes and, soon, Robert Mitchum, little could have prepared him to marshal the army required to make a feature film in six weeks, plus care for an ailing parent.

At the time, Danny was on a roll: the year before, he had made his directing debut with the English television film *Mr. Corbett's Ghost*, a supernatural tale co-starring his father and the noted British actor, Paul Scofield (*A Man for All Seasons, The Train* and, later, *Quiz Show*). As 1987 began, Danny had just finished *Bigfoot* for the Disney television series. He went from that to *Mr. North*.

Continuity is a cornerstone in show business. Certainly, when it comes to employment, one form of continuity—jobs—is critical. But there is another kind of continuity, and that is the theatrical tradition: "The show must go on," "Never give the public a bad performance," "Never let them see you sweat," and so forth. On occasion, families form dynasties as more than one generation embarks on careers on the stage or screen: the Booths, the Barrymores, the Redgraves, the Bridges, the Sheens, the Douglases, the Quaids, the Carradines, the Keaches, the Hemsworths, and a lot of Baldwins. Among the *Mr. North* company, Mary Stuart Masterson is the daughter of director Pete Masterson, while Tammy Grimes is the mother of actress Amanda Plummer, her daughter by Christopher

Plummer. But the dynasty that sends them all back to the gene pool is the three generations of Hustons. By appearing in his son's first theatrical feature, John was merely doing for Danny what his own father, Walter, had done for him in 1941 in John's first theatrical feature, *The Maltese Falcon*. It was Walter Huston who made an unbilled appearance in that now-classic mystery; he played the messenger who dumped the fabled black bird into Humphrey Bogart's lap just before collapsing. Of course, Walter Huston was later directed to an Oscar® by son John in 1948's *The Treasure of the Sierra Madre*.

Likewise, Anjelica Huston was introduced to films by her father in a tiny role in *Sinful Davy* in 1969, was raised to co-star in that same year's *A Walk with Love and Death*, and was directed by him to her own Oscar® in 1985's *Prizzi's Honor*." Her participation in *Mr. North* is further proof of the dynastic Huston clan's penchant for helping one another.

With the elder Huston in Charlton Memorial Hospital, however, the torch was yet to be passed. On the set on the second day, Danny waited apprehensively while discussing the script.

"There was an earlier draft[1] that was given to me by a company in Los Angeles," he recalled between camera set-ups and phone updates from the hospital. "I liked it because of the dialogue and the great characters in the piece, but it needed a major rewrite." That was the version that producer Steven Haft had discovered while he was confirming his acquisition of the project, which had made its way to the young Huston through his agent.

Fortunately, Danny knew of a competent rewrite team. "I approached my father and Janet Roach," he explained, noting that the last time the two had collaborated was for *Prizzi's Honor*, whose script received an Oscar® nomination. "They immediately liked the script and set to work. They combined the book, the original script, and themselves. The thing the book lacks is a tight plot, which is essential for a film."

Janet Roach remembered, "[John] called me one Saturday morning in April and said, 'How soon can you get out here, Honey?' I said, 'Well, I'm having some people to dinner tonight, John.' He said, 'Oh, well, fine. Come in the morning then.'" At the time, Huston and Roach lived across the country from each other.

The Huston-Roach friendship had begun when Roach was making Bill Moyers' television show and did an episode on Huston.[2] Some time later, she was visiting the director on a boat in Los Collator when he hand-

---

1. By James Costigan (q.v.)

2. *Creativity with Bill Moyers* (1982)

ed her a first draft screenplay of Richard Condon's novel *Prizzi's Honor* and asked her for an appraisal. "The next day I did," she said, launching into a Huston impression. "He said, 'How'd you like to try your hand at rewriting this, Honey?' That was it. I had directed and written documentaries for ten years or so, so it wasn't like I was completely unorganized. But nobody except John would've done that."

When it came to revising *Mr. North*, Huston and Roach wound up shaping a screenplay that was almost a literary achievement in its own right, turning Wilder's sprawling, reserved novel into a comedy of manners so delicate that it bespoke a long-gone style of filmmaking.

"It does have a sort of reverent quality of how films were at one time," Danny wistfully agreed. "I like that elegance, especially for my first picture."

Roach explained the collaborative process which she and Huston developed: "I'd work by myself until two or three in the afternoon, and then take John the pages that I'd done that day, because we only had six weeks to write the script. Then we'd go over what I'd written and I'd do it again. John is very strong on structure, but he'd never use the word. He wants to have (she lapses again into a Huston impression) 'a beginning, and a middle, and an end, Honey.'"

Whenever an additional writer is brought onto a project, the Writers Guild of America conducts a compulsory arbitration to determine final screen credits. Thus *Mr. North* wound up with the credit: "Screenplay by John Huston & Janet Roach and James Costigan." The WGA uses the ampersand [&] to signify a writing team and the word *and* to show that another writer followed the first two. The fact that Costigan preceded, rather than followed Huston and Roach, suggests the vagaries of the controversial WGA arbitration process.

Danny Huston embodies another form of vagary: his upbringing. "I'm not really sure where I'm from," he joked, noting that he had spent his life traversing the Atlantic Ocean, and then some. "I spend half my time in Los Angeles and half my time in London." He did, however, feel comfortable on a movie set; after all, he had twenty-five years of visits to his father on such diverse locations as Morocco, Hungary, Africa, Mexico, and anywhere else the elder Huston sought to shoot.

"American film crews have a sort of snazzy quality about them," Danny observed. "Just in the way they start up a take. They'll say, 'Scene Charlie, take two' where the British will say a simple, 'Scene C, Take two.' Americans say 'rolling' and the British say 'turning.' Apart from those superficial things, either a crew is good or a crew is not good, and this one happens to be very good." After a few days, many of the Yanks even started to say "turning."

"There haven't been any problems," the soft-spoken Danny continued, "so I don't feel the need to shout at anybody. But if the moment comes, I'll do my bit.

"Film is a large organism. What a director tries to do is keep everything in harmony. When everybody's doing his job correctly, the energy virtually fills the place."

What inspired young Huston, and it was palpable, was his love for his father. In an era, and an age, when many sons felt the need to repudiate their parents, Danny was the opposite. "I have such good opportunities and I seize them. I use every little bit—any time I can drop my dad's name more, I don't hesitate! I think I'll make my dad proud with this. I hope so. Yet I don't feel any competition with my father. He was writing scripts at my age. He's been helping me—I go to give him a full report of what's happening, and I try to keep the questions brief. He just asks if I'm okay. He also asks questions over and over again making sure I'm saying the truth!"

When John Huston started writing in 1932, he was a contract employee at Warner Bros., which released one film every week and encouraged, even threatened its writers to turn out material. The film industry has changed considerably since then; as producer John Houseman once stated, "In the old days they used to help a producer make a film, now they dare him."[3]

"There's a lot of good stuff out there, but it can't get produced," Danny agreed. "I've got a few things in mind which I'll start working on when this is finished. Leon Garfield, who wrote *Mr. Corbett's Ghost*, has a new book I'm interested in. I'm interested in doing a murder committed through pure evil." He half-closed his eyes and savored the thought. "I've got a little mean streak in me."

As it would turn out, Danny forsook directing after 1996's *The Maddening* to concentrate on acting, quickly receiving more acclaim for his thespic abilities than his father ever had. At the time of *Mr. North*, in fact, Danny was beginning to question how public a life he should pursue, in light of perception that he was riding on his father's and sister's considerable coat-tails. "I wonder," he said in a private moment. "I don't feel any. One person who makes me feel I should have started younger was Steven Spielberg, who directed when he was younger than I was. But I do very

---

3. Conversation with the Author, circa 1979.

little to relax. I think about film every day whether I'm relaxing or not. I collect features on video; my idea of a perfect afternoon is watching three or four films, one after the other. I love art, particularly painting, and I try to paint, too."

Like his father, he was also peripatetic. "I've got friends all over the world, but I don't really know where I live. When I'm not working, I'm insecure with getting something else going. It takes seven months to get something happening: lunches, meetings, more meetings. The meetings are where Dad is the best help. You get Dad into a meeting and it only lasts a couple of minutes. There's no waste." He recalls an experience that repeats the apocryphal meeting between an experienced director and an arrogant studio tyro who wanted the director to recite his credits: "a kid asked a question about the script, about plot and meaning. Dad just waited a moment and said to him, 'Tell me something about yourself first.'"

8

Robert Mitchum

The word they used most often to describe Robert Mitchum was *laconic*. It means "brief; expressing a great deal in a few words." That description, too, is laconic. There is another word that people used to describe him, people to whom he chose not to show his charm, or who weren't seduced by it when he did: *difficult*.

Robert Mitchum was both. This was a man who was said to have checked himself out of the Betty Ford Clinic so he could go drinking. Who respected the craft of acting until somebody complimented him on it, then joked, "I got three expressions: looking left, looking right and looking straight ahead. People think I have an interesting walk. Hell, I'm just trying to hold my gut in." He despised the press, yet gave them permission to talk about his fights, his drinking, and his jail time by challenging them, "They're all true: booze, brawls, broads, all true. Make up some more if you want to."

Were these contradictions? Hypocrisies? Textures? With Mitchum it could have been all three at once.

He was also an absolute original, a man in whom the muse ran so deep that he pretended not to possess it. Out of that conflict came his art as well as his turmoil; he never reconciled the two. When he agreed to substitute for John Huston in *Mr. North* he was 70 and had come to be regarded as Hollywood's most obstinate leading man. Fiercely private, secretly poetic, gregarious at times and combative at others, he long ago paid his tab and had come to understand that he would never be acknowledged as the great screen actor he was. He also hated the press with a passion that came to be returned in kind. In fact, the press had fired the first shot in 1948 when the then-RKO contract player was arrested for smoking marijuana at a party at actress Lila Leeds' house, and the newspapers ran out of ink writing about it.

"I dunno what it was all about," he once said in a television interview. "I went to a party, I walked into a room, somebody handed me a joint, I went 'whfffffff' (inhaling sound) and What! It was the cops."

Burned or not, Mitchum harbored coldness for the journalists whom most actors find it to their advantage to court. His attitude toward this reporter was no exception. "Talk?" he challenged during as break in *Mr. North*. "What's there to talk about?" and returned to his newspaper. Five minutes later he moved his canvas chair to the shade, within the stone wall of the mansion, into an area patrolled by security guards.

His arrival at Newport had been late at night. Touching down at Boston's Logan Airport, where photographers had been tipped off about his flight, he ignored them and rushed by car to confer with Danny on location an hour's drive away. He'd had little sleep, and practically no time to study his lines for the next morning's (Wednesday, July 28) 8 AM call. Before registering at the Sheraton in Newport, Mitchum stopped by Charlton Memorial Hospital to see his old friend. He and Huston had first worked together in 1957 making *Heaven Knows, Mr. Allison*, in which Mitchum played a Marine stranded on a Japanese-controlled Pacific island with a nun, played by Deborah Kerr. It is one of his most grizzled performances, and a film shot through with gusto. Huston and Mitchum got along famously, but their schedules did not bring them together again until 1963's *The List of Adrian Messenger*. In that mystery, which starred George C. Scott as a sleuth chasing a seemingly unrelated sequence of deaths, Mitchum appeared in a cameo part wearing completely unrecognizable makeup.[1] It was stunt casting and symbolic of the playfulness that the two rough-and-ready friends felt toward each other, right straight through to *Mr. North*.

What the rest of the cast did not know was that Huston had slipped a copy of the script to Mitchum a week earlier. "It was a precaution," producer Steven Haft admitted, acknowledging that Huston was worried about not being physically up to performing the Bosworth role himself.

---

1. Reports have emerged since then that the heavily disguised guest stars in *Adrian Messenger* (Tony Curtis, Kirk Douglas, Frank Sinatra, Burt Lancaster, and Mitchum) were actually Dave Willock and Jan Merlin and only appeared as themselves during the final unmasking. Another Huston prank, perhaps?

Thus, when Mitchum became John McHenry Bosworth, while ABC-TV obligingly shuffled his *War and Remembrance* scenes to accommodate his mission, he was not as unprepared as people thought.

Although, he did have to learn a 96-page screenplay in one day.

Confirming Mitchum's presence, producer Skip Steloff beamed as much with pride as with relief. "He was one of a group of major, stellar actors who wanted to take this job. He was John's first love for it. At the hospital last night when we told John of Mitchum's coming here, he breathed a sigh of relief and said, 'That's terrific.'"

Equally pleased, if still worried, was Danny. "I'm very interested to see what he does with the part," he offered tentatively. "But we won't need a rewrite. After all, this is a John Huston script."

And what would be the first thing Danny planned to say to Mitchum on the morning of their first day of work?

"Action," he smiled.

In point of fact, one slight rewrite was necessitated by Mitchum's presence: Bosworth's age was changed from Huston's 80 to Mitchum's 70.

When Mitchum took his place behind Bosworth's heavy wood desk in the dark, book-lined study of Chateau-Sur-Mer, it was as if Huston was hovering. That was because Mitchum was able to perform an uncanny impression of John Huston. As the camera crew aligned the lights in the tiny room, and cinematographer Robin Vidgeon briefed Steadicam® operator John McNeil on how to use the floating camera to represent Theophilus North's point of view as he enters Bosworth's study, Mitchum sat down with Danny and script supervisor Karen Golden. Anthony Edwards also met Mitchum for the first time as they ran their lines.

"It was a simple 'good morning' and we went right in," Edwards reported.

Even though film acting is more subtle than stage acting, it still requires an immense amount of energy and concentration. Imagine a painter who has to cover a huge canvas with a small brush and that's a fair idea of the complexity of movie acting. When film actors perform, they allow their emotions to surface, and the camera has the ability to photograph them. No one knows how it happens, but it does. When the emotions are false, of course, it also photographs those.

When actors "run lines" it is not a true rehearsal; it is, literally, repeating the lines out loud to confirm them in memory and also to let the other actors know what everybody's voice sounds like reading the cues.

Actual performance level will be set when the scene is "put on its feet," that is, physically staged.

To loosen the proceedings, Mitchum ran his lines as John Huston. Huston was his paradigm. As the film went on, Mitchum would make the part his own. Unfortunately, the first scene he shot was also the audience's first meeting with Bosworth, and so the mold would be set before it was fully formed. Because of this pressure, everyone cleared the library so that the actors and director could work in privacy. Besides, everybody wanted to talk about Mitchum's surprise arrival.

"John is such a man of honor," offered co-writer Janet Roach. "He knew it was a risk taking this part, and his sense of honor told him he had to protect the film. He had talked to Mitchum about stepping in."

Mitchum's rumbling voice could be heard echoing through the silent hallways of the Chateau, and they possessed Huston's lilt and cadence. Janet Roach acknowledged that, "I wrote some of the lines for John's mouth, using his phrasing," but she denied that Mitchum was "doing" Huston. Meanwhile, the rehearsal progressed.

"Come in. And shut the door," he says to Edwards. "I'm John McHenry Bosworth."

"Theophilus North, sir," Edwards responds with a slight bow. The two characters feel each other out, as do the two men. North is a Yalie; Bosworth attended Harvard. North admits he was being sarcastic with Bosworth's daughter; Bosworth admits she deserved it. Then, to seal the deal, Bosworth rises and offers North his hand.

"All right, then. Two hours, three days a week. Shake on it?" he says.

Suddenly "TN" (which is how the script abbreviates "Theophilus North") seems reticent. Rather than take Bosworth's hand, he shuffles his feet in what looks like a ceremonial dance, and touches the desk lamp.

"What's this all about?" Bosworth asks, mystified.

"It's nothing, sir," TN tells him. "It's just that . . ."

"Well?"

"Well, sir, it's my body. I have an extraordinary capacity for building up electrical charges. Sometimes when I touch people I shock them."

"You're speaking metaphorically," Bosworth says, dryly.

"Oh, no, sir," North replies in utter earnestness. "It seems I'm a walking Tesla coil."

Mitchum paused. "You're a walking testicle?" he asks, amazed.

For an instant, Edwards was not sure what he'd just heard, and if he did hear it, what was he going to do about it. Then Danny laughed and everyone loosened up.

"Is that really what you said?" asked Mitchum. "You're a walking *testicle*?"

"That *is* sorta what it sounds like, isn't it?" Danny chuckled.

"That's okay," soothes Mitchum. "I did some reading on Nicola Tesla. He did early work in electricity, and then they took it all away from him. Stole everything."

Some observers near the set look back and forth, amazed that the actor who never seemed to care about anything should have cared so much. But Mitchum did not acknowledge. Meanwhile, he looked at the props, including the book he was about to hand Edwards. It was supposed to be *A Treatise Concerning the Principles of Human Knowledge* by Bishop George Berkeley. Mitchum already knew of Berkeley beyond the script's identification of him as "an Anglo-Irish philosopher, 1685-1753."

"Is this pronounced *Bark-ley* or *Burk-ley*?" the actor asked.

"*Bark-ley*," script supervisor Karen Golden offered, preserving the English pronunciation.

"What, do the kids in California go to *Bark-ley*?" Mitchum jabbed.

"It's like *Kay-ro* Illinois and *Kye-ro* Egypt," said Roach. "In England they have a *Temz* river but in Newport there's a *Thaymz* Street. You figure it out."

Mitchum harrumphed and sniffed, "So here my father's name would be *Thom-muss*?" (as in "thumb").

"Yes," says Roach.

"No shit."

While Mitchum returned to rehearsal, Roach confided, "I've had a crush on Mitchum ever since I saw *Heaven Knows, Mr. Allison*. And I don't know why he's never received his due as an actor. He's a literate, intelligent, and informed man and I think he'll put the world into this."

Edwards, too, felt excited. "I feel very, very fortunate to be working, period," he joked. "But to be working with *him* is a tremendous opportunity. I'll learn a hell of a lot in the next six weeks."

Except, of course, to be laconic or difficult.

9

Huston Watch

Everyone is worried. A newspaper for Thursday, July 30—the first full day that Robert Mitchum worked as John Huston's replacement—reports that Huston's medical condition had been downgraded from "good" to "serious." A shaken Steven Haft confirms only that Huston continues to recover in the hospital's intensive care unit.

Ernie Anderson forces himself to be optimistic. "People have been counting him out for decades," he repeats. "He's like a tombstone: too tough to die."

Syndicated columnist Liz Smith further mitigates the newspaper's report:

> Huston was reported to be in good condition this morning by a hospital spokesman. Mitchum, who can sight-read and learn lines at a glance, is a natural for the Huston role. This heroic "save" by Mitchum is in the actors' tradition of always stepping into the breach like the real pro he is. And the company will work fast to finish his scenes in *Mr. North* because Mitchum, who will be 70 next week, must report in mid-August to finish *War and Remembrance*.

But the truth was that nobody knew the truth. Huston, in declining health through complications from his chronic emphysema, was not, it turned out, "rushed" to the hospital. He was, instead, driven there after making arrangements with Doctors Nicholas Mucciardi and William C. Sheehan to supervise his stay. Huston's companion, Maricela Hernandez, went with him, and he was met there by ex-wife Zoë Sallis (Danny's mother) who had been present throughout the early stages of the production.

"As long as he doesn't get pneumonia, he's all right," Anderson repeated.

By the end of the week, he had pneumonia.

Production manager Tommy Shaw was brooding. He probably knew the director better than any man on earth. He had done his bidding for nigh onto thirty years. Wiry, grey-bearded, standing about five nine, he was never seen sitting, and looking like a leprechaun who lost a fight, Shaw commanded the forces for Danny's film, just as he had for Huston's since *The Unforgiven* in 1960. He knew what might happen to morale if, after all this, Huston never showed up on the set.

"I've been doing this all my life," Shaw said while rushing between the mansion location and nearby Salve Regina College where the caterer was setting up to serve lunch. "I was a child actor and then a one-man gang with David O. Selznick in 1935. I was fifteen. In those days, they didn't call 'em 'gophers'. I would go for coffee, go pick up the mail, help the secretaries . . ."And now he was helping the caterers. There was already some grousing from cast and crew about the food. Said Lauren Bacall, "I may hard boil some eggs and bring them. The chicken today was still walking."

Bacall's presence inspired a certain attitude from the crew and cast members. A famous beauty in her teens when she was placed under personal contract to director Howard Hawks, Hawks starred her opposite Humphrey Bogart in *To Have and Have Not*, creating a romance as well as a classic. She was both aloof and earthy, and could be both feminine and gruff. This was, after all, the woman who tamed Bogart into calling her "baby." Born Betty Jean Perske in New York City in 1924, Bacall seemed amused when people, presuming familiarity, called her "Lauren." As anyone knows who knows film lore, Bacall's friends call her "Betty." This day she was pushing her salad around the plate. Union rules ordinarily specify that a hot meal of at least two choices of entrée be served within five hours of the call time. The *Mr. North* caterer was dishing up salads and cold cuts. The health-conscious California contingent started a revolt which the easterners threatened to join. It was Shaw's job to squeeze better food out of the film's budget, or at least out of the film's caterer.

Shaw, for his 67 years, remained combative. He remembered one of his earliest films, the now-classic *Nothing Sacred*, for Selznick, with Fredric March and Carole Lombard. He was 17 at the time and remembered, "I still had to go to school then, so I wasn't a delinquent."

His first job with Huston, after years of hearing stories about him, was when he was assigned by the Hecht-Hill-Lancaster production company to lend a hand at *The Unforgiven* location. It was a star-studded western in which two Indian tribes go to war over Audrey Hepburn. Lillian Gish also appeared (about whom more later).

"First day of shooting," Shaw recalled, "we're doing a scene where Hepburn comes out of her house and goes to get some water. And while we were back in medium long shot I said, 'While we're back here, why don't we get her exit?'"

"He [Huston] just said, 'That is not the way I shoot pictures.'"

"What the fuck do I say?" Shaw asked rhetorically. "He then said to me, 'When we're on a close shot, that's when we'll do her exit.'"

"So, later in the day, the wind starts to blow. I don't really know him very well. He talks dropping this sequence and going to Joe Wiseman, who plays a loony bastard, and talks about doing it in the wind. But we won't be on schedule; who knows when the wind'll blow again? I said to myself, 'How are we ever gonna be able to schedule this thing? I know we don't have a wind machine; we're in Mexico.'"

"Well, I know an American who runs the airport, went to the airport and got these two Cessna airplanes. Now I know I'm gonna [be able to] make the wind shot. Only I don't tell him.

"The next day the producers are in the car and I'm with John. We're about to go to lunch and, before we go to lunch, I say, 'John, I want to show you where you can do the scene tomorrow with Wiseman blowing around.'

"He says to me, 'How do you know the wind's gonna blow tomorrow?'

"I said, 'I don't know, but I don't care, we'll make it blow.' I don't tell him how yet.

"So we go to the location and, believe me, there's a Joshua tree here, there's a Joshua tree there, it all looks the same. So I said, 'You can do it here.'

"He says, 'It doesn't look the same.'

"I say, 'Yes it does.'

He says it doesn't, and the producer says, 'What the hell difference does it make? The wind's gonna blow anyway.'

"We have this argument, we get in the car, the producer says, 'God damn it, that's wrong,'

"I say, 'fuck you, it's not wrong, it's the same fucking tree.'

"All of a sudden John turns around. He always sits in the front seat. He says to the producer, whose name was Jim Hill, 'you know, we're both full of shit. He's absolutely right.'

"From that moment on, I don't know what I've told him to do, for thirty-some-odd years, he's done it. I never left Huston."

Very few people had more perspective on the Huston directing style than Shaw.

"In all the years I've known him, I never heard him tell an actor or an actress that it was bad," Shaw recalled. "Ever. On that particular picture (*The Unforgiven*) Lillian Gish was over the top; she was back to D. W. Griffith, back in the old silent days, and it was one of the most important scenes in the picture. Every time we'd go through it, he'd tell her how great it was and that he'd like to do one more. Well, we did 75 takes on it until he wore her completely out. When she could hardly talk, we did one more when she was exhausted, and she was great."

Shaw's loyalty to Huston carried over to Danny. In a way, it was like going back in time; here is another Huston making pictures. Yet Shaw also knew that Danny had to progress at his own pace, that he was not the father, and that the film business was not the same.

At the same time, he was worried about John. The conflicting news reports didn't help. On a single day (Sunday, August 2) there were three:

"Oscar®-winning director John Huston is responding to treatment for pneumonia, his doctors in Fall River said yesterday, but he is expected to remain hospitalized for several weeks."
– *The Boston Globe*

"His condition is still considered to be serious, but he has demonstrated daily improvement."
– *The Providence Journal*

"The legendary Oscar®-winning director John Huston is in serious but stable condition at Charlton Memorial Hospital in Fall River, Mass. where he was taken after an emphysema attack on his way to film a role in a new movie."
– The New York Post

In all, Huston was variously reported as being seriously stable, confined to the intensive care ward without visitors, and still working on the film while responding to treatment after an emphysema attack, which left him both bedridden and walking around with pneumonia. By this measure, Huston was a man of many talents.

By Monday, August 3, his condition was upgraded to "fair," inspiring hospital spokeswoman Dorothy Allen to announce, "We have plans to celebrate his 81st birthday in the intensive care unit on Wednesday," while refusing to confirm that Huston had been taken off his respirator. Nobody asked whether he had ever been put *on* a respirator. But it demonstrated the continuing interest that people maintained in *Mr. North*, even if it was morbid interest. On the set, there was little time for conjecture. For the actors and crew it was not 1987, but 1926, and, despite those who tried to crash the set seeking tidbits, nothing inside betrayed the artifice.

Mitchum learned his Bosworth lines and wanted only to deliver them to Anthony Edwards with the authority of his character—as Bosworth, finally, not as Huston. In the story, from their tentative acquaintance, Bosworth and North become friends, and that friendship helps North liberate Bosworth from his wood-paneled prison.

Between takes, Mitchum explored the desk that was provided by the combined skills of art director Eugene Lee, set decorator Santa Nathanson, prop master Robert H. Schleinig, and his assistant Randi Savoy. Most fascinating to the actor were several issues of H. L. Mencken's *American Mercury*, the literary magazine of the 1920s that gave early voice to countless prominent young writers, among them John Huston. Although there are three 1925 *American Mercury* issues on the desk, none contains a published Huston manuscript.

"We did try to find one," Schleinig says. "It would have meant something to Huston if he'd seen them."

The sixty-year-old periodicals nevertheless attracted attention from those present, even if the audience may only see them in the corner of the frame. One thing they will never catch is a framed oil portrait of the man who built Chateau-Sur-Mer, William Shepherd Wetmore. Mitchum, however, did see it, and studied it with the concentration of an artist. There was no physical resemblance; Wetmore was slight while Mitchum was stocky. But the actor was drawn to an irony in the name in that, in the story, Bosworth is confined to his home because of incontinence. "No wonder they called this guy *Wetmore*," the actor cracked.

Between takes, stretching his long legs, Mitchum was relaxed.

"I never see dailies," he announced, bowing out of the nightly ritual of watching the previous day's footage. "I did once. It was a big picture at MGM and they'd tarpaulined off half the studio for the set, and it had Van Johnson and everybody in it. Clarence Brown, the director, who had started with Garbo, asked me to be there, and I went. It was this touching scene and everybody watching the dailies was crying. And there in the back is Harry Stradling, the acclaimed cinematographer, who's going, 'There's this damn dog in the third race. . .' We're supposed to be looking at the stuff we shot yesterday, and he's checking off a racing form! So that's the artist for you."

Able to sight-learn his lines, Mitchum cautioned writer Janet Roach that some memory-challenged actors might not be so accommodating if told that their carefully practiced lines were going to get last-minute revision. Roach disagreed.

"What do you mean?" Mitchum teased. "You've changed the script three times since this morning!"

"Just little changes," she held her ground. "You can handle 'em."

"You try that on Cary Grant, he'd be gone for a week."

"Not lately."

"No, not lately," Mitchum agreed, begrudgingly, (Grant had died the year before). "Lot of actors, you change a script, they go home. You think it's to study their lines, but they're at the track. They are gone—G-A-W-N." Then he himself left the room.

Assistant Director Tony Cerbone called for Mitchum to take his seat again, this time to feed lines to Edwards for Edwards' close-ups. Mitchum would not be on camera, and even his dialogue would be pulled from previous takes. Yet Mitchum returned to cue Edwards, realizing that their face-to-face interaction would benefit the young leading man's performance, and thereby the film as a whole. This was unusual. Stars of his stature often balk at hanging around once they have been released, that is, they are no longer the center of attention. When he stayed, it only increased the respect that everyone felt for him, and overcame the memory of his earlier sullenness.

10

On a Roll

Because Mitchum changed his schedule to meet *Mr. North* halfway, *Mr. North* changed its schedule to meet Mitchum. As the second week of filming got under way, Mitchum and Edwards shot a scene which occurs much later in the story—one in which Bosworth, outfitted with rubber underwear provided by North, drives into town. The location scouts found a long driveway leading up from Bellevue Road to the Van Buren estate that had hardly aged over the past fifty years, and that photographed on film (as long as no modern cars drove into the shot) as timeless. This was a boon for the company. Rather than go through the effort of removing the television antennas and street signs which bespoke modern times, all the camera had to do to evoke the 1920s was keep up with the actors.

Edwards and Mitchum spent all morning pretending to ride in a chauffeured vehicle that was, in reality, being dragged by a camera car back and forth along the same driveway until Danny got what he wanted.

The 1920 Rolls-Royce belonged to local motor enthusiast Ted Leonard, and he had maintained it in pristine condition. In the story, Bosworth has not set foot outside his house in eight years, so his car looks as polished as Leonard himself has kept it. Mitchum and Edwards enjoy the ride from the back seat of the open car while Danny and Robin Vidgeon squeeze next to Leonard in the front, whose shotgun seat had been removed to accommodate them. That didn't leave any room for Bill Randall and his Nagra tape recorder so, for the set-ups in which the riders are seen in long shot, dialogue would have to be looped (dubbed) in post-production.

Randall was even less fortunate when it came time to do the close-ups. He and his son, who wielded the overhead boom, had to balance on the car's running boards, hanging on for dear life while the vehicle wound along the tree-shadowed road. Grips carefully mounted the camera support on the car's side fenders; even with padding, this still made Leonard nervous. It turned out that he was right to be fussy; on one take, the car lurched, throwing the camera operator against the front window of the Rolls convertible. The glass was only cracked, but by the time the accident showed up in the next day's newspaper, the poor operator had sailed through the broken glass and out the front of the car, and sustained injuries.

"Gee, I'm sure if it had happened, I'd have heard about it," chuckled Ann Shaw (Tommy's daughter), who is in charge of the production office. "Because I would've had to fill out the insurance forms!"

Fortunately, the public was barred from the next accident: lunch.

Once again, it was cold salad time at the Salve Regina College lunch room. This time, the caterer (who was not connected with the school, which was on summer session) augmented his now-traditional cold entrees with chilled pasta. The only thing icier was his reception. But a free meal is a free meal, and Lauren Bacall, who would not be needed in front of the cameras for another week, showed up anyway to visit co-stars Anjelica Huston and Virginia Madsen. Her presence at a rear table caused assistant director Tony Cerbone to walk over.

"If you're going to have lunch with us every day," he said politely to the regal Bacall, "let me know so I can tell them to add you to the count."

"I'll be here," she replied with one of the world's most famous voices and reached into a nearby ice chest for a fresh bottle of Perrier.

Lunch on location is catered in a single sheltered area, but the people eating it tend to gather within their job cliques. This has nothing to do with status, only the fact that the way a film crew is scheduled to work sends different departments to their victuals at staggered times. Actors generally get first crack at the food (well, behind the Teamsters, but that's another story), followed by make-up, costume, grips, and gaffers. The assistant director and production manager grab a sandwich. And the camera crew is lucky to get there when there is still desert left. The director hops from table to table checking on the next set-up and upcoming scenes.

Actor-painter Martin Mull once said that "Hollywood is like high school, with money," and everybody knows how important the lunchroom is in high school. More than anything else, lunch is the company's chance to spend half an hour away from the curious eyes of the public, for their sheltered feeding area is fiercely guarded. In quite another way, the artifice of movie making is also fiercely guarded. No matter how many behind-the-scenes TV shows purport to reveal Hollywood's technical secrets, it is still impressive to watch them at work. For example, the mansions of Newport posed both plusses and minuses. The plusses were that they were real, were gorgeous, and displayed an authenticity that no set designer could possibly match inside a soundstage. The minuses were that they were made for people, not camera and lighting equipment, and rigging them for movies was a mechanical nightmare for the ultra-skilled Hollywood crew. The photography was made easier by the availability of newer, faster color film stocks that didn't need as much lighting as in the old Technicolor days, and current digital technology has cut that even further. But the cramped rooms dictated the use of wide-angle lenses that may compromise the "classical" look that the filmmakers originally wanted.

On the other hand, nobody had to redecorate the fabulously ornate building façades, polish the paneled walls, fluff the plush upholstery, or accent the ceiling filigree. They were the real thing.

There were also movie tricks used by the expert craftsmen to create illusion. For a shot where an actress had to be peer through a lace-curtained window, the prop department rigged a false window in the open driveway and draped a café curtain in front of the frame, which didn't have any glass in it (so there would be no reflections). Shot in tight close-up so the camera couldn't see past the edges, it easily cut into interior shots filmed earlier, and saved the need to lug cameras and lights inside to a real door. A simple moment when an antique limousine glided up the gravel driveway was ruined because the camera crew was reflected in its polished black door. The age-old movie gaffe was solved when a prop man applied a coat of a coat of dulling spray to the door while assuring the skeptical owner that it was washable.

No matter how well-rehearsed the actors and camera moves may be, every movie take is, by definition, different. Script supervisor Karen Golden made meticulous notes in her copy of the script, which, by the end, becomes so full of annotations that it is called a "lined script" and becomes indispensable to the editing process. Golden—lean, bright, and supernaturally observant—sat below the camera and noted every nuance of the shots: when an actor changed dialogue, which hand he used to pick up a prop, what line he said on standing or sitting, and so on. Her written index, which included slate numbers, lens readings, and myriad Polaroids for continuity purposes, would form the "bible" that film editor Roberto Silvi would consult in assembling the finished sound and picture.

Every time a car or bicycle tire crossed the gravel driveway, its tires left fresh ruts. They are exactly the kind of thing that astute moviegoers like to count and scream "flub!" So, between every take, a crew member used the back of a garden rake to smooth the gravel to its grooveless state.

When Anthony Edwards pedaled his bicycle to the door of the mansion, he arrived with perspiration on his face. The July heat in Newport was hot, but not that hot, so to create the illusion of exertion, the well-rested Edwards got his face spritzed with water by the make-up man.

Every film is made the same way. Every film is different.

Writer William Goldman (*Butch Cassidy and the Sundance Kid, All the President's Men*) famously wrote that the most exciting day of your life is your first day on a movie set, and the most boring day of your life is your second day on a movie set. Imagine being on a movie set for a living. Thus, when plans started circulating that Wednesday, August 5 was going to be a celebration of John Huston's 81st birthday, it not only broke up the dreariness, it restored a sense of excitement. A small, quiet observance was being attended by family members, and award-winning photographer Kal Roberts, who had been retained by the producers to create custom, period portraits for the production, would record the event to allay rumors of Huston's failing health. No one else would be admitted, even though the whole world wanted to know.

"People are sending flowers from Ireland, France, and Los Angeles, and they have a rule at the hospital that no flowers are allowed in the intensive care ward," Ernie Anderson fretted to the *Newport Daily News*. "We always have a big party. I don't think we can have a party this year until he comes out of the hospital. Then we'll have a delayed birthday. You can't do much in intensive care. But he's getting lots of mail and good wishes from friends, and also from fans."

Press statements to the contrary, Danny Huston was nonplused. "Dad and I don't care about birthdays," he said. "We don't even call each other for them."

11

Mitchum at 70

The day after John Huston turned 81, Robert Mitchum hit 70. In a way, it was like hearing that Shirley Temple was drawing Social Security. Not that stars don't grow up—technically speaking, when you watch their old movies, they don't—but it's just not something you like to think about. As Norma Desmond might have said, stars are ageless, and Mitchum's image was of the rowdy, ageless S.O.B. who could take care of himself and hang out till all hours with the best of them. His screen roles celebrated that vigor: *El Dorado, Cape Fear, Thunder Road, The Sundowners, The Story of G.I. Joe, Night of the Hunter,* and certainly John Huston's *Heaven Knows, Mr. Allison* bubble with immortal virility.

"Bob's problem," offered a female co-worker, who later wondered if the word *problem* was accurate, "is that, in addition to being such a great actor, he throws off an enormous sex appeal from the screen. That always kept people from appreciating his talents."

He also has other, more refined qualities. "Robert Mitchum is a classicist," Ernie Anderson pronounces as the sun rises orangey over the Budget Motor Inn. "Last night at Christie's, one of Newport's most popular restaurants, he had, before dinner, three double Tanqueray Martinis, and spoke in great detail about whether the proper dry Martini is six, nine, fourteen or twenty-three parts gin to vermouth.

"Anyway," he continues about the actor who completed a well-reported stay at the Betty Ford Center three years earlier, "he was intelligent to order doubles. Straight up, with a twist and an olive, both. Instead of dithering about whether to have a drink, he just *did*."

After cocktails at Christie's, the Mitchum party launched into a good Sancerre wine, lobster bisque, lobster salad and clams, all of which the gruff Mitchum finished, and then skipped dessert.

Classic.

"If he's seventy years old, he's a very good seventy," Anderson admired.

Born in Bridgeport, Connecticut and educated in New York City's public school system, Mitchum married at age 23 and four years later landed his first movie acting job in a Hopalong Cassidy western. Westerns and Mitchum remained pardners through the intervening years. He even eternally wedded his voice with the cattle industry through a series of TV commercials touting "beef: it's what's for dinner."

But his contemporary roles often proved more interesting, from the wife-killer whose son wanted him dead in the underrated *Going Home* (1971) to the retired hit man who helps a friend in *The Yakuza* (1975), to the world-weary gun-runner who double crosses the wrong hood in *The Friends of Eddie Coyle* (1973). He was miscast in David Lean's *Ryan's Daughter* as a meek schoolteacher (Mitchum? Meek?) whose inattention drives his wife to adultery. Other gambits included private eye dramas (a fine *Farewell, My Lovely* in 1975 and a needless remake of *The Big Sleep* in 1978) and a handful of television appearances (*The Winds of War* and in a few episodes of *The Equalizer*, for which he stepped in for Edward Woodward just as he subbed for Huston). He even attempted the film version of Jason Miller's Pulitzer Prize-winning play, *That Championship Season* in 1982, although his somnambulant performance offered only a shadow of his former vitality. It was almost as though Mitchum was searching for the legitimacy that had long escaped him while, at the same time, rejecting anyone who dared to confer it upon him. That duality characterized the tough actor throughout his *Mr. North* gambit. Moody, private, ornery, yet also funny, supportive, and self-critical, but never generous, Mitchum remained impenetrable.

The complexity of the man was never better demonstrated than when he paid a visit to the hospitalized Huston on August 9. Stopping by the room as though he only happened to be in the building, Mitchum boosted Huston's spirits as one scalawag would admire another.

"John, you suckered us all," Mitchum told the ailing director. "Come on, stop faking it and get out of bed."

Mitchum went on to accuse Huston of wanting him to take the role of Bosworth all along, and feigning illness just to lure him east. Huston returned the laughter. "That's right! This is the greatest hoax I ever perpetrated." Then he asked, in tones that one pro reserved for another, "How's Danny doing. I mean, how's he *really* doing?"

Mitchum leaned over to whisper in Huston's ear. "He's doing a good job."

Huston was so moved by his friend's pronouncement that his eyes grew misty. He then bade Mitchum a quick goodnight and watched him walk from the room. Mitchum paused casually at the nursing station to get the attention of the attendant on duty.

"There's blood on his neck," the star told the nurse. "It looks like something cut him, or the I.V. tube came out. Don't alarm him, but see what you can do."

The nurse rushed off. The intravenous shunt had, indeed, come loose. Mitchum stayed until Huston was stabilized, then quietly left. Only the first part about the visit reached the set.

12

The Sweat Box

Orson Welles once joked that a film director was someone who presided over accidents. He was referring to the climate of anticipation and uncertainty that hovers over a movie set under which, if the director is lucky, something special happens during a take that brings it to something larger than life. Aside from such inspiration, film productions don't look forward to accidents. That is why care is taken on planning.

If only the Newport weather went along with the plan. The second week of August, ordinarily the hottest and most humid of the New England summer, held to tradition. The company was shooting in and around the town's historic Colony House in Washington Square smack in the center of town. The two-story wooden structure once housed the state Supreme Court and, for the climactic courtroom scene in the picture, was filled with over 100 costumed extras appearing as townspeople gathered to witness a sensational trial: Dr. McPherson (David Warner) versus Theophilus North for practicing medicine without a license.

North's celebrated static charge gets him in trouble with the local quack when he somehow effects a cure for young Elspeth Skeel's (Mary Stuart Masterson) migraines. His accidental success draws ailing Newporters to him in cultish devotion, threatening the local medical establishment. North is hauled before Judge Cadwalader, the role for which Burgess Meredith was originally cast and which, upon Meredith's withdrawal, was held open for John Huston. Obviously unable to leave the hospital, Huston was once again replaced, this time with an actual judge: Thomas Needham. Needham not only sat on the Rhode Island bench for real, he achieved international recognition when he presided over the second trial of Klaus Von Bulow when the socialite was charged with the attempted murder of his wife, Sunny. Needham acquits himself with an authoritative performance, but his voice will nevertheless be replaced by another actor by the time the film is released.

Sharing the "courtroom" with Needham were the extras, principal actors, Danny's crew, and the thousands of watts of light needed to fill the corners of the historic location with enough candlepower for Robin Vidgeon to put images on film. Regardless of how bright the daylight was outside, the shifting sun over the course of the day would create changing shadows, so the candlepower had to be boosted to smooth the illumination. This scene was the dramatic payoff, and it had to come off well.

The problem with bringing so much light indoors is that the windows had to be closed and covered with sheets of darkening neutral density filters, and the electric lights inside raised in strength and color temperature to match the daylight. That, plus the weather, turning off the ceiling fans and over 100 costumed extras, meant that the temperature in Colony House climbed to sweatbox levels. If criminals ever sweated in front of Judge Needham, on this day the Judge himself did, too. And so did everyone else. Even when the fans were turned on between takes and the doors were opened, it was an ordeal.

A lounge was set up in the jury room where the principle actors could sit in front of fans. The extras milled around on the first floor, never straying so far that they could not hear their call to re-assemble inside.

David Warner, who played Dr. McPherson, was reading a paperback book in his jury room seat between takes. Internationally known for his iconoclastic performances in *Morgan, Tom Jones, Time Bandits, Time After Time,* and later for playing Leonardo DiCaprio's and Kate Winslett's omnipresent nemesis Mr. Lovejoy in *Titanic,* the British Warner stole his scenes in *Mr. North* as the arrogant society quack who was mortified by Theophilus North's charming guilelessness. Warner's book was James Agee's collected essays, and the particular piece that the actor was studying was, *The Undirectable Director,* Agee's acute portrait of Huston. As it had with Janet Roach, the quality of Agee's work attracted Huston's attention, and, in 1950, Huston would ask him to adapt E.M. Forster's *The African Queen* for him to direct in 1951. Warner was impressed.

"To be asked to work with such wonderful people, especially the Huston family, is an honor," the actor enthused in his polite, soft voice that seemed worlds apart from many of his screen portrayals. This was not the first time he worked with Huston, however. "I was in *The Bible,* but only my voice!" he said. "I was brought onto the dubbing stage and they used my voice for Adam [played by Michael Parks]. That was the only working experience I had with John Huston before this, but the way things are in this business, people always run across one another. This is a nice little role in a lovely little project, and to be included in it is very nice."

Warner commented on the disparity between his actual demeanor and the quirky roles he has often played. "I've never thought of myself as a flamboyant actor. I always thought I was a bit of a bumbler. It's just the way I've been cast. Jack the Ripper (in *Time After Time*, a fantasy in which writer H.G. Wells chases Jack the Ripper from Victorian London to modern San Francisco in the time machine) was one of those roles. I mean, you don't want to try to create sympathy for him, but you do get the feeling that when he gets back into the time machine at the end, and Wells (played by Malcolm McDowall) pulls the plug out, that he knows what he's doing and wills it that way.

"Of course, I want to play more kinds of people, but somehow you have to do this. I'd love to play, well, not the heavy—I thought it was just the American system, or Hollywood, but now it seems to be universal. One does tend to get into a rut of roles, but let's face it; some others I know get tired of playing good guys."

Having made his screen debut in films directed by such British "angry young men," as they were called, as Tony Richardson and Karel Reisz, Warner commented that "My friends from England seem so ask me to be in their first films. But I've also worked with Joseph Losey, Alain Resnais, Sam Peckinpah, Sidney Lumet, and Arthur Hiller. I've been used by the masters, and that allows me to work with the young people. Some of my friends in England have been honest enough to tell me, 'help me, I don't know what I'm doing.' Nicholas Meyer (writer-director of *Time After Time*) said the same thing: the worst thing a director can do is come on like he knows everything. We're all there to help."

Careers rise and fall in capricious ways, too. "I remember on *Time After Time*, Malcolm McDowall had had one line in my *Hamlet* in England and the next time I met him, he's the movie star about to marry his leading lady (Mary Steenburgen). You can't get much more 'Hollywood' than that!"

One experience that Warner treasured was custom-made for him: *Providence*, the 1977 drama starring John Gielgud, Ellen Burstyn, Dirk Bogarde, Elaine Stritch, and himself. It was the dark story of a dying writer (Gielgud) who imagines the end of his next novel as an intertwining series of relationships drawn from his life and fantasies. Directed by Alain Resnais, it was written by David Mercer. "Resnais asked David Mercer, who had written *Morgan*, to write a script for me, John, Ellen, Elaine, and Dirk. It took him six months to a year. David would write ideas and we'd develop them. By the time we shot, it was perfect."

Providence became a hard-to-see cult classic. "It was a dream," Warner explained. "It's not often a screenwriter gets the chance to write a script from scratch knowing who his actors are. At one time I wanted to add the word *no* to a line and Alain Resnais, the director, said, 'We'll have to call the writer.'" A founding member of the French New Wave, Resnais was one of the screen's most respected but least linear filmmakers. Such films as *Last Year at Marienbad* and *Hiroshima Mon Amour* attest to his daring, and sometimes confusing, artistry. "I haven't been able to understand all of Alain's pictures," Warner admitted, "but [*Providence*] comes closer than most of them to something I can comprehend."

How did *Mr. North* compare? Warner was enthusiastic but realistic. "This is a lightweight picture," he said, describing the film without a hint of condescension. "I don't play Dr. McPherson as sinister and awful. I go the other way. I play him as one of those pompous, arrogant people who gets his comeuppance. He has a line in the trial sequence we're shooting: 'We can't have a situation where people go around curing each other without us!' That about sums it up, doesn't it? I don't mean to denigrate doctors, but they are paid an awful lot of money, aren't they? Then, again, so are movie actors."

Warner reopened the Agee book and found his place, then looked up wistfully. "I'm usually playing characters who are on their own. I would like to show that six-foot-two-inch characters can also be in love." He smiled tightly. "It would be fun to play James Bond."

Across the actors' lounge, resting while Judge Needham's close-ups were filmed in the courtroom, sat Mark Metcalf. He had arrived in a suit jacket and tie for his role as Mr. Skeel (Elspeth's father) but, instead of trousers, he was wearing shorts. His shots for the day were all close-ups, and Metcalf wanted to be comfortable. When he was not sitting with Mitchum or Harry Dean Stanton, he, like Warner, was trying to catch up on his reading. If Metcalf was not widely recognized by his actual name, he was better known by the name of a character he played in a low-budget comedy he made in 1978: Douglas Nedermeyer, the fascist R.O.T.C. commander in National Lampoon's *Animal House*. Ten years gave the personable, and decidedly non-fascist, Metcalf some perspective on what its meant to be in a quickie comedy filmed in Oregon, and that went on to become one of the top-grossing, in any sense of the word, movies of all time.

"It was eight weeks," the actor recalled. "We all worked for scale (SAG minimum) except for John Belushi. They gave [director] John Landis some points after it hit, I'm told, but it wasn't like *Star Wars* where George Lucas gave some of his own points away to his people, even though he didn't have to. We kind of thought it would have been nice to get points," he said with a tinge of sarcasm in his resonant voice.

After *Animal House*, Metcalf turned producer with Griffin Dunne and Amy Robinson to film what became a cult classic, *Head Over Heels*, the screen version of Ann Beattie's novel, *Chilly Scenes of Winter*, about an obsessive love affair. He also acted in it to save money. In *Mr. North*, he continued acting in a role vaguely reminiscent of the Nedermeyer bearing. He echoes David Warner's feelings about typecasting. "Hollywood is of such limited imagination that they think of you that way. I did a rock video for Twisted Sister as that character—just for fun. That typed me, too! But it's kind of interesting. Yes, Nedermeyer. All of us achieved a certain kind of immortality because of an eight-week period in Eugene, Oregon."

Inevitably, any conversation about *Animal House* sooner or later turned to John Belushi. "He was living hard even then," Metcalf reported with a touch of sadness. "John earned his death every day."

An endearing feature of Metcalf's in *Animal House* legacy is what happened to his character after graduation, summed up in the film's "where are they now" end sequence. The various tags reveal that one student became a Beverly Hills gynecologist, another, a sensitivity trainer, etc. Nedermeyer's says he was killed (fragged) by his own troops in Viet Nam. The joke caused conniptions at staid Universal Pictures. "It was 1978," Metcalf/Nedermeyer recalled. "The war was long over, but, still, Universal Studios had not faced up to it. *The Deerhunter* was being made by them, so to say about a character in a comedy that he was killed by his own men was too heavy. They lobbied heavily with John Landis to change it. But Viet Nam was my character's main motivation. It was a film very much about the country being in the 1950s, much as it is today. My character represented the government end of it—the R.O.T.C. guy—and the helmet I used was the same helmet that George C. Scott used in *Patton*; they rented it from Twentieth Century-Fox (*Patton*'s studio)—for a price. And quite a price it was, too." The tag stayed in, as fans of *Animal House* know.

Having produced a political documentary on Nicaragua just before joining the *Mr. North* company, Metcalf brought with him a vision of his character as a mover for social change in 1926 Newport. "He is very much a symbol of upper class Victorian society, but he departs from it. The morality of some of the people of Newport in the story is juxtaposed with the people of the Jazz Age. North enters the scheme and he changes it by confronting it. The Skeels are part of this change; once they go over, so does Newport society. Skeel represents the coming generation, the second generation of wealth."

There was also another kind of society present: filmmaking society. Metcalf looked around the room and remarked, "There's legends everywhere around here. I'm old enough not to be impressed, but still—." His eyes rested on David Warner. Metcalf leaned forward. "His film, *Morgan* (the 1966 British hit about a nonconformist artist who tries anything except sanity to win back his estranged wife) saved my life. If I hadn't seen that movie and gone back half a dozen times, I wouldn't have known it was all right to be insane. I was an engineering major in college, then did drama. *Morgan* told me it was permissible to be around the bend."

One happy note as the day's filming progresses at glacial speed: the caterer started serving hot lunches. The crew and principal cast had its choice of two cooked, steaming selections. Ironically, with the temperature inside the courthouse reaching 100 degrees, most opted for cold salads. But at least the seditious battle cry, "This wouldn't happen if the old man was here," meaning Huston, was no longer being whispered among the troops.

13

The Acting Judge

"**H**ell, I think I know the script better than you guys do right now," Judge Thomas Needham ruled from the Bench. Needham, as Judge Cadwalader, got to preside over the stars, extras, and crew of *Mr. North* while keeping order in the trial of Anthony Edwards, a.k.a. Theophilus North. Unlike his usual domain, this time Needham had to follow the orders of a man half his age: director Danny Huston. Still, the jurist regarded the film as a pleasant way to spend his summer vacation. He even beamed when he could correct his young director on a point of dialogue.

"That's *his* line," Judge Needham pointed out, stopping a take (a huge Hollywood no-no) to correct a point. In Hollywood, only the director may say "cut."

"I'll start to blush soon," Danny admitted, letting it go.

"Let's be serious," begged assistant director Tony Cerbone, who was trying to keep the show on schedule. "After all, there's a Judge here!"

Cinematographer Robin Vidgeon, Danny Huston, and script supervisor Karen Golden positioned themselves at strategic spots around the room, taking empty seats where the stars would be sitting, and read the lines aloud to help the Judge make the proper eye contact for the editing process.

It was only 8:25 in the morning, but it must be 90 degrees so far in the room, and soundman Bill Randall was turning red.

"It's all I can do to keep the sweat from rolling down in my eyes," he griped.

Danny was giving the Judge direction. In the scene, he will have his character deflated by Mrs. Cranston (Lauren Bacall) who will admonish him, "Nicholas!"

"You probably had an affair with Mrs. Cranston at some time and you don't want it to come out now," Danny suggests. The dignified jurist is game, especially considering the elegant Bacall. "It's all right if you want to fix me up!" he joked, but warned, "I've never had anybody use my first name in a courtroom before."

But after several takes Danny still had not gotten the reaction he wanted. "Pretend you're gay and this is a man," the director whispered. "Be more startled that Cranston is here—play a little more shock." The director knew that the revelation would be a good laugh, but after three more takes, he leaned over to Karen Golden.

"Can we cut it with his look? " he asked her. She shook her head "no." Danny called for take six.

"Too much," he said at the Judge's over-broad next attempt. "You moved your head too far; you'll sue us for whiplash."

Take seven was perfect. The judge looked relieved. "Takes a hell of a lot of work, my friend," he decreed after his acting debut. "I had some reservations about this, to be honest. But I'm on vacation. And I'll tell you, off the record, that I've never felt less in charge in a courtroom before!"

Did the crowd of extras make Judge Needham, the man who fended off the international media when Klaus von Bulow appeared in his Court, nervous?

"No," he smiled impishly. "I'm used to playing to packed houses."

14

Missing Huston

While the courtroom scene was shot, the cast and crew showed their affection for the absent John Huston. Karen Golden arranged with a local printer to rush-produce a box of shamrock green lapel pins which sported, in white lettering, "Happy Birthday John Huston." They arrive at the courthouse reading instead, "Happy John Huston Birthday," but everybody behind the camera sported one for the day.

Downstairs, the extras chipped in to buy a remembrance: a teddy bear outfitted with a leather vest. It was delivered to the ailing director at his hospital room. Newport radio personality Jeanne McGregor was the instigator of the *ad hoc* ursus. Like a good reporter, she also infiltrated the production; after having been repeatedly thwarted from getting interviews with the stars, by landing a job as an extra. Production personnel admired her resourcefulness, but were unyielding in refusing interviews. It remained a closed set and none of the outside press, not even a visiting reporter from the *New York Times*, could win more than a cursory nod from anybody.[1]

At the hospital, the only non-family member allowed to see Huston was photographer Kal Roberts. This time Roberts arrived with Anjelica, Alegra (just over from England), Danny, and Zoë to snap a birthday photo which was then devoured by the wire services. When it appeared in the papers, it was treasured by cast and crew alike. It might be indiscreet to report that a certain number of glasses containing "a wee bit of the creature" were raised to Huston's health, but it would be entirely proper to report that, if such a thing even was done, it was done after work hours.

---

1. At times like this, it's nice to have an exclusive. Especially as a Freelancer.

The hospital had, by this time, instituted a daily report on Huston, as worldwide media continued to call for details.

Today there were none to be had.

All anybody was told was, "John Huston is improving."

But the truth was that he was not.

Theophilus North (Anthony Edwards) bicycles from mansion to mansion in Newport, Rhode Island, circa 1926 (photo: Kal Roberts)

Anjelica Huston as Persis Bosworth-Tennyson (photo: Kal Roberts)

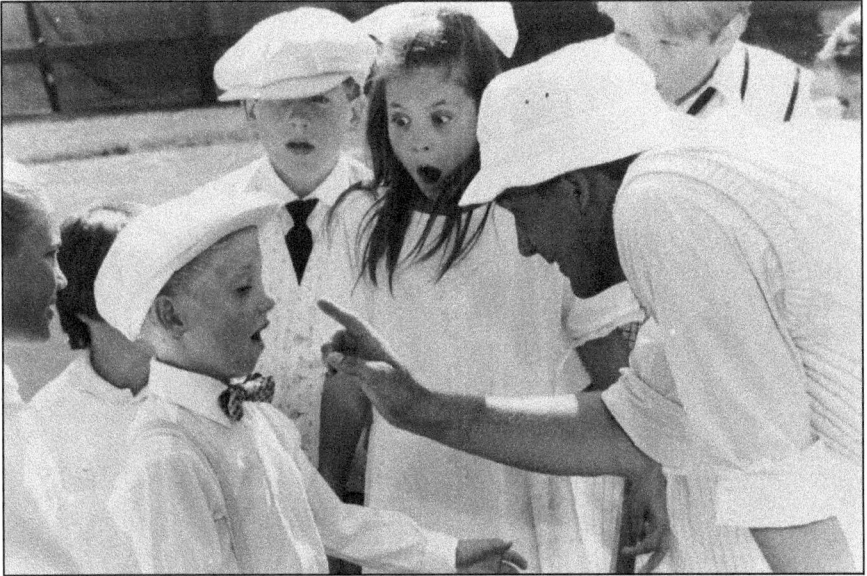

Theophilus North (Anthony Edwards) interrupts a tennis lesson to show children his "special gift" of static electricity. (Photo: Kal Roberts)

Robert Mitchum appears as James McHenry Bosworth, a rich man being held
homebound by a medical condition. (Photo: Kal Roberts)

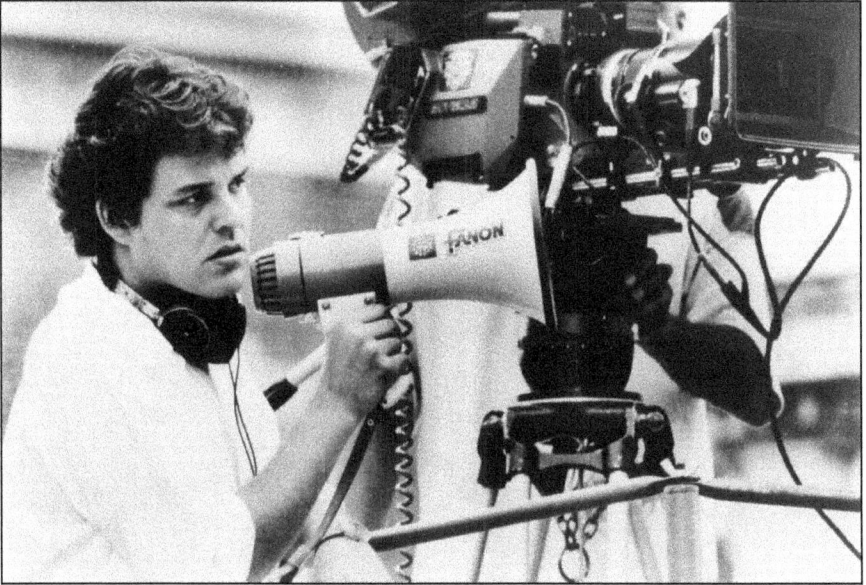

Danny Huston directs his first theatrical feature. (Photo: Kal Roberts)

Lauren Bacall (Amelia Cranston) and Harry Dean Stanton (Henry Simmons) attend the trial of Theopholus North. (Photo: Kal Roberts)

Danny Huston laughs at something Robert Mitchum has said on the set of *Mr. North*.
(Photo: Kal Roberts)

John Huston

Chateau-Sur-Mer (photo: Skip Plitt - C'ville Photography)

John Huston

Thornton Wilder, author of *Theophilus North*, in 1948 (photo: Carl Van Vechten)

William Shepard Wetmore, who built Chateau-Sur-Mer (photo: James Carnahan Wetmore)

Danny and Anjelica Huston attend the 62nd Academy Awards on March 20, 1990 (Photo by Alan Light.)

TOMORROW Free CASH IN THE MARKET stocks

FOR TODAY'S LUCKY WINNERS, SEE PAGES 5, 14 and 24

Boston Herald

WEATHER
TODAY: Showers. High in the 60s
TOMORROW: Partly sunny. Highs near 75.
Details on Page 20

TODAY'S TV: Page 39

Telephone (617) 426-3000 ★ 25 Cents 35¢ BEYOND 35-MILE ZONE ® Saturday, August 29, 1987

John Huston, a H'wood legend, dead at 81

By ROBERT CONNOLLY and NAT SEGALOFF

JOHN HUSTON, the legendary director who vaulted to fame on the strength of a series of hard-boiled Humphrey Bogart thrillers, died in Rhode Island yesterday where he worked on his final film, "Mr. North."

At Huston's bedside, according to sources, were his companion, Maricela Hernandez, and her sister. He reportedly had smiled at them, raised both fists in a clasped prize-fighter's victory sign, and slipped away.

Huston's ex-wife, Zoey, the mother of Danny Huston, who is making his directorial debut with "Mr. North," also was present, sources said.

The Oscar-winning director's death at age 81 was attributed to complications resulting from chronic emphysema.

Yesterday, as word of the famed director's death rippled through the film's Newport, R.I., base, the cast and crew awaited word from Danny Huston. By 9 a.m., the word was out — keep working and finish the film on schedule.

"Danny made the decision himself," said a production source. "He's doing no more than John Huston would have done."

Earlier this week, the elder Huston had visited the "Mr. North" editing room and was shown most of the rough cut by his son and editor Roberto Silvi. Production sources reported that Huston had been "very, very pleased" with the film.

He had also attended an equestrian show in Newport last Sunday.

A free-spirited direct-

Turn to Page 2

JOHN HUSTON, above, the Academy Award-winning director who thrilled generations of moviegoers with such films as 'The Maltese Falcon' and Prizzi's Honor,' died yesterday at age 81. He is shown at left with actor pal Humphrey Bogart during filming of 'The African Queen.' More photos, stories: Pages 2, 3, 16 and 17.

Airlines agree to end delays

Feds warn: Be on time or pay fine

By ED CAFASSO

SIX MAJOR airlines yesterday reached an agreement with the government to end the delays that have irked travelers at the nation's four busiest airports, including Logan International.

By Nov. 1, Logan passengers should see flights on American, Delta, USAir, United, Continental and Eastern airlines take off within 30 minutes of their published schedules 50 percent of the time or more.

And by April 1, the airline's flights will operate within 30 minutes of their published

Turn to Page 6

Aquino: We'll deal harshly with traitors

MANILA, Philippines — A grim and angry President Corazon Aquino yesterday branded as "monsters" the rebels who tried to topple her government and said they will be dealt with harshly.

"I have nothing to say to these traitors," she said on independent

Turn to Page 4

CORAZON AQUINO
Calls for unity

first page: The August 29, 1987 front and inside pages of the *Boston Herald* announce John Huston's death. (Courtesy of *The Boston Herald*)

The Boston Herald, Saturday, August 29, 1987 **3**

PASSING OF A FILM LEGEND

Remembering 'the master'

By NAT SEGALOFF

NEWPORT, R.I. — Calls of sympathy flooded the production offices of "Mr. North," where legendary director John Huston was working before his death yesterday.

"He was a landmark in film history, a great friend, and I'll miss him very much," said actor Michael Caine, who along with Sean Connery worked with Huston in "The Man Who Would Be King."

Robert Loggia, who co-starred in "Prizzi's Honor," said, "Working with John Huston was a unique experience as an actor.

"He worked with the cast like a master conducting a symphony. He generated a feeling of love and loyalty. I had the same devastating feeling when my father died. They both passed away from emphysema. 'Prizzi's Honor' should go on his epitaph and I hope it will go on mine too."

In "Prizzi's Honor" Huston directed his daughter, Anjelica, to a Best Supporting Actress Oscar. Thirty-seven years earlier, Huston directed his father, actor Walter Huston, to a Best Supporting Actor Oscar for "The Treasure of the Sierra Madre."

After learning of Huston's death, Mickey Rooney said, "The Sierra Madre has lost its treasure."

Huston's screenwriting partner, Janet Roach, said, "John had room in his heart for so many people of all kinds."

Calls were coming into the company's production offices from all over the country expressing sympathy. One was

from Huston friend Ava Gardner, who was at one time supposed to play a role in "Mr. North." The part was later taken by Lauren Bacall.

Actor Anthony Edwards, who plays the title role of Mr. North, termed Huston's death "a tragedy. This is the saddest day of the year."

Added Huston's longtime production manager, Tom Shaw, "He was the original 'macho man' — you can tell by his films. I can't tell you how much he meant to me. He was a huge part of my life. Everything really good that happened to me in this business was caused by him."

LAST BIRTHDAY: John Huston was forced to celebrate his final birthday from a hospital in Fall River. But his family, clockwise from lower left, daughter Allegra, ex-wife Zoe Sallis, son Danny, and daughter Anjelica, were there to celebrate with him.

Huston touched the entire company of "Mr. North" even though he never set foot on its set to act, as originally planned. He was, instead, taken to the Charlton Memorial Hospital in Fall River July 28, where he was diagnosed with pneumonia complicated by chronic emphysema.

On the set yesterday it was "business as usual," but no gesture or thought was far from John Huston. People hugged one another instead of shaking hands and looked at each other as though being guided by the ghost of the man.

Their focus was Danny Huston.

Turn to Page 17

A glimpse at an elusive genius

UNHAPPY CALL: Actor Anthony Edwards, who plays the lead in 'Mr. North,' waits outside Newport, R.I., YMCA for start of shooting yesterday. Staff photo by Jim Davis

Editor's Note: Nat Segaloff was the only reporter allowed on the set of John Huston's last film, "Mr. North." He was granted a rare interview with Huston shortly before the legendary director's death.

By NAT SEGALOFF

Although The Herald was granted unprecedented access to the set of "Mr. North," access to John Huston, the co-writer, actor and executive producer, proved more elusive.

Huston, hospitalized on the second day of shooting, remained unavailable to anyone but family members and close production associates.

I did, however, have a chance to meet the legendary Huston on the Sunday prior to the cameras' rolling — two days before he would be hospitalized. It was in his rented house, Sea Meadow, overlooking Newport Harbor.

I was introduced by Er-

nie Anderson, Huston's publicist and a close friend for 30 years. In the kitchen, Huston's companion, Maricella Hernandez, was preparing lunch for

Verniere chronicles Huston's life: Page 16

the players of a poker game then earnestly in progress in the sunroom.

Sitting around the broad table were actor Harry Dean Stanton, Steven Haft (co-producer of "Mr. North"), Michael Fitzgerald (producer of Huston's "Wise Blood" and "Under the Volcano"), film editor Roberto Silvi ("The Dead") and, of course, the man himself.

Even ravaged by age and disease, Huston looked tall in his chair. Dressed loosely in house-clothes, he was contemplating whether to bet or

check on a game of "Hold 'Em" that Stanton had just dealt.

It was impossible not to notice the clear plastic tubing that ran from the center of the house, winding through the hallway and living room, down three steps and into the poker room, ending beneath Huston's nose. It was the oxygen passing through this tube that kept him alive.

Huston was known as a gambler — thousands at a time — and in this heady crowd, the fives and tens were intimidating.

"Bet's to you," Haft reminded Huston, who contemplated a raise. "OK," he said, "I'll go 10."

Stanton was next. "Ten?" he confirmed. "Well, OK, count me in. A

dime." So much for high-stakes poker.

Huston's appearance at this game was striking, if not shocking. White-haired, groomed informally (it was, after all, a Sunday), he seemed to lose focus occasionally until brought back into the proceedings.

Yet he was also unfailingly polite, remarked how well Ernie looked, and exchanged pleasantries about the film, about the articles we'd do, and the success he ho_ed his son, Danny, would have with "Mr. North."

Thornton Wilder — who wrote the novel on which Huston's final script is based — once noted that it is those tiny, day-to-day events that define the truth of a person's life. We usually think a man is measured by drama and crises. Yet it is those small pieces of time that speak more eloquently than all the dramatic moments ever could.

second page: The August 29, 1987 front and inside pages of the *Boston Herald* announce John Huston's death. (Courtesy of *The Boston Herald*)

2 The Boston Herald, Saturday, August 29, 1987

NEWS / IN BRIEF

U.S. mulls use of floating barges as bases in Gulf

MANAMA, Bahrain — The United States, frustrated by the refusal of Persian Gulf nations to provide it permanent support bases, is considering using offshore barges as floating bases in the region, sources said yesterday.

The 400-foot-by-100-foot barges would be lashed together and anchored in the northern Persian Gulf as base camps for mine-sweeping helicopters and boats and beyond range of Iran's silkworm missiles overlooking the Strait of Hormuz, sources in Washington said.

The Navy used barges as support camps more than a decade ago in Vietnam.

Three states send killers to deaths

THREE convicted killers went quietly to their deaths yesterday while a fourth got a last-minute stay on the busiest day for the death penalty since the Supreme Court allowed states to resume executions in 1976.

Wayne Eugene Ritter, 33, convicted in a pawnbroker's murder, died in Alabama's electric chair.

Pierre Dale Selby, 34, convicted in the "Hi-Fi" torture murders of three people and the maiming of two others, was executed by lethal injection in Utah.

Beauford White, 41, who stood guard while six people were shot to death in a robbery at a suburban Miami home, was electrocuted at Florida State Prison near Starke.

30 homeless in $100G Lynn blaze

LYNN firefighters rescued several people from an apartment building blaze yesterday that left 30 homeless and caused $100,000 in damages.

Lynn Fire Department Capt. John Elwell said the eight-unit apartment building on Franklin Street was fully enveloped in flames and smoke when he arrived at the scene about 8 a.m.

Officials and one Lynn firefighter, Wyane Wilkins, suffered smoke inhalation, and one dog was killed in the fire.

13 dead in two Contra attacks

MANAGUA, Nicaragua — Eleven Sandinista soldiers died and nine others were injured yesterday when their Soviet-built MI-17 helicopter was hit by a U.S. Redeye rocket fired by Contras, the Defense Ministry said.

Two other Sandinistas died when Contras ambushed their jeep, the ministry said.

The helicopter was transporting Nicaraguan army troops between Zompopera and La Vigia in Jinotega province, the ministry said.

Two-car crash hurts 8 in Foxboro

A TWO-CAR crash at a problem-plagued intersection on Route 1 in Foxboro yesterday sent eight people to the hospital, State Police said. Five were being held overnight.

Margaret Fisher, 32, of North Attleboro was traveling northbound on Route 1 when her car was hit by a car turning onto the highway from Pine Street, said Foxboro Trooper Dermot Moriarty.

Fisher and her two children, Gayle, 8, and Adam, 4, were taken to Norwood Hospital. Adam was held overnight for observation.

The operator of the second car, Janet Ferris, 42, of Wrentham was traveling with her parents, Whadia Ferris, 70, and Ferris Michael Ferris, 73, her sister, Jean Jordan, 46, of Arizona, and her niece, Tracey Jordan, 17.

Janet, Jean, and Ferris were listed in fair condition at Sturdy Memorial Hospital, Attleboro.

Whadia and Tracey were taken to Norwood hospital where Tracey was treated and released, and Whadia was listed in fair condition.

Vietnam 'may have found' GI remains

BANGKOK, Thailand — Vietnamese authorities may have discovered the remains of three American servicemen listed as missing in action, a U.S. delegation sent to negotiate aid to the country said yesterday.

Lt. Col. Joe Harvey, head of the delegation, said Vietnamese officials also provided information about Americans believed captured by communist forces during the war.

Compiled from wire and staff and wire reports.

PASSING OF A FILM LEGEND

John Huston dead at 81

From Page 1

or, writer and actor, Huston was the creator of such film classics as "The Maltese Falcon," "The Treasure of the Sierra Madre," "Key Largo" and "The African Queen."

Huston, who lived near Puerto Vallarta, Mexico, directed 40 films during a 46-year career.

The crusty filmmaker publicly rued his longtime habit of cigarette smoking in recent years. He was almost continually tethered to an oxygen bottle because of his respiratory woes.

Haft said the death occurred at 2 a.m. and that family members and crew were notified before the police.

Producers working on the film said in a statement that Huston's body would be returned to Los Angeles for burial.

Huston had been released Aug. 19 from Charlton Memorial Hospital in Fall River after he was hospitalized for three weeks for emergency treatment of his illness. He was ordered to continue physical therapy and medication.

Before he was hospitalized, he had been on his way to play a role in "Mr. North," a movie directed by his son, Danny, and co-starring his daughter Anjelica. He was forced to turn over the role to Robert Mitchum, but planned to remain as executive producer.

Huston, in his rich,

deep voice, once repeated his own father's advice: "Don't work at anything simply for money. Choose your profession as you would choose your wife: For love — and not for money."

"Recently I heard myself described as a living legend," he remarked upon receiving an award for his achievements in 1985. "My doctors assure me that the first wintry blasts would almost certainly change my present status."

In a long and adventurous career — as action-filled as the films he made — Huston caroused with Humphrey Bogart and Ernest Hemingway, broke his nose in a fistfight with Errol Flynn and directed Clark Gable in his last film.

Huston said he was never quite sure how to describe the stories that attracted him as a filmmaker. "I suppose it has to fulfill me somehow," he once told a Boston Herald reporter.

"If there's a pattern to my work, it's that I haven't made any two pictures alike. I get bored too quickly," he also said.

Huston gave minimal direction to his stars. "He feels, for the kind of money we get paid, we ought to know how to do it ourselves," Michael Caine said.

Of his hands-off directing, Huston also said, "I try to get the most out of him (an actor) by directing just as little as possible."

FAMILY TRADITION: Director Danny Huston, son of John, walks into Newport, R.I., YMCA after hearing of father's death. The young director, shown going over father's script for 'Mr. North' with Robert Mitchum in file photo below, decided to continue shooting on the film yesterday. *Staff photo above by Jim Davis*

INDEX

Advice	32	Jumble	35
Arts	26-30	Living	31
Bridge	20	Lotteries	71
Business	21-24	Movie Lists	30
Bus. Opportunities	43	Obituaries	40-41
Classified	42-65	Racing	65-69
Comics	34-36	Sound Off	41
Cross Clue	34	Sports	66-80
Crossword	35	Television	37-39
Cryptoquotes	34	Tops on TV	39
Editorials	18-19	Trivia Quiz	34
Horoscope	20	Weather	20

The Boston Herald

©1987 News Group Boston Inc.

THE FAR SIDE   By GARY LARSON

Tough spiders

Calling The Boston Herald

Teleservice	426-3000
Circulation/Customer Service	426-9100
Classified Advertising	423-4545
All other business	426-3000

---

third page: The August 29, 1987 front and inside pages of the *Boston Herald* announce John Huston's death. (Courtesy of *The Boston Herald*)

The Boston Herald, Saturday, August 29, 1987   17

PASSING OF A FILM LEGEND

SMILE OF SUCCESS: Huston smiles over success of 'Prizzi's Honor' with cast of the 1985 film, from left, Jack Nicholson, Kathleen Turner and daughter, Anjelica Huston.

Actors reminisce on a craft master

From Page 3

ton, John Huston's 25-year-old son, the film's director, who opted to continue production in the same spirit his father would have wanted.

Huston had known many of the key production personnel from what is now his last completed film, "The Dead," which features his daughter, Anjelica.

Speaking of her father at the time of his hospitalization, she said, "He's been on so many adventures; he relishes adventure. It's the fine line between what you fear and what makes your heart beat faster, and I think he's a man who has gone for the rush of adrenalin in his time."

Bacall, who first met Huston through her then-husband, Humphrey Bogart and later worked with them both on "Key Largo," said at the time; "He instills great trust, which is the best way to direct. He has a great gift for that, and when you

trust your director, you feel you're able to try anything, because you know he will always stop you when you're going too far."

Having worked with Huston on what will now be his final contribution to the art of film, screenwriter Roach revealed that she had sensed a feeling of satisfaction in her partner just before his death.

"He had seen all of his children get launched — Anjelica won the Oscar for 'Prizzi's Honor' and that was a great moment for him; he was very proud of Danny; Tony had written a script that John was pleased with (for 'The Dead'); and Allegra is successful in publishing in London.

"His last words to me, when he'd seen the footage last Monday (of "Mr. North," run specially for him), were, 'Very good, Honey.' When we were writing 'Prizzi's Honor' I lived for those words. I got a lot of them: 'Very good, Honey,' " Roach said.

TEAM EFFORT: Huston, left, hams it up with father Walter after winning 1949 Oscars for 'Treasure.'

fourth page: The August 29, 1987 front and inside pages of the *Boston Herald* announce John Huston's death. (Courtesy of *The Boston Herald*)

15

The Living "Dead"

Anjelica Huston invited everyone to stay after dailies to watch *The Dead*. Completed by her father only six weeks earlier, the special screening was as much to gauge everybody's reaction as to thank those on the *Mr. North* crew who had been fortunate enough to have worked on *The Dead*. No one knew at the time, although everyone silently suspected, that *The Dead* would be the last film that John Huston would ever direct. But, before *The Dead*, the dailies for *Mr. North*.

Few Hollywood rituals have survived the upheavals of business, technology, or style as the screening of dailies. This raw, unedited, unadorned footage, sometimes called "rushes," represents the first time people connected with a production can see on a big screen what was shot the day before. Today, when digital photography has replaced film and everyone gathers around a "video village" to watch a scene moments after it is shot, it's good to remember the importance of old-fashioned dailies. Seeing work on a big screen is the only way to check for mike shadows, flaws in makeup, costume malfunctions, and the myriad minutiae that one cannot always catch on a video monitor or laptop playback.

Different departments use dailies for specific reasons: actors judge their performances, and sometimes become so self-conscious that they skip further viewings; costume and make-up experts check how their work looks on camera; cinematographers evaluate their images; editors note what shots they still need in order to construct the finished film. Beyond that, the crew gathers to share the experience and the memory of their recent achievement while there is still time, in some cases, to re-shoot and correct mistakes. Put another way, dailies are the world's most expensive home movies.

Within the studio system, there is a hierarchy of who gets to see dailies, and when. Production executives get first crack at them, particularly if the crew is on location. Sometimes two sets are made: one for the moguls back in Hollywood, the other for the people who are actually making the movie. Now that dailies are uploaded for streaming onto encrypted servers, the pecking order has somewhat changed. But, in the case of the independent *Mr. North* in 1987, the producers were already on location and the nightly showings offered a way for people to squeeze into the Old Newport YMCA after wrap to hang out and, from the corner of their eyes, try to see if the producers were happy.

This was no plush Beverly Hills screening room. Instead, a screen was stretched between a couple of pillars in the Y's cramped auditorium which, by day, served as indoor mess hall. Nearby was Silvi's editing room where he and assistants Keith Sheridan and Alan Jacques tried to stay ahead of the incoming footage. Separate reels of picture and sound track were rolled into neat cores. (In a very few years, the intricate filing system of a film editing room would be replaced by purring computers.)

The old Y, reprieved from the wrecking ball long enough to headquarter the film, also served as warehouse for the film's scores of period costumes, the set for where Theophilus North takes lodging, and, each evening, became a screening room. Everybody was invited to sit in rickety folding chairs or on the hard floor to watch the work unfold.

"A movie never looks as good as it does in dailies or as bad as it does in rough cut," said Anthony Edwards, quoting Francis Ford Coppola as he grabbed a soft drink. Added Janet Roach, more comfortingly, "If they laugh at the dailies, they'll laugh in the theatre." Actors like Mitchum and Bacall do not bother with dailies. They know what they look like, and they have been doing it long enough. Others such as Edwards, Mark Metcalf, Virginia Madsen, Harry Dean Stanton, Tammy Grimes and Mary Stuart Masterson came to see their and everybody else's work. Danny Huston, Robin Vidgeon, Roberto Silvi, and script supervisor Karen Golden made furious notes during the dailies for later review, just as Danny and Silvi would pore through the footage scores of times before the film is finished.

Dailies offer approbation and admonishment. Watching his work as Dr. McPherson, David Warner heard the applause of his co-workers who were delighted at his expert range of facial expressions that wordlessly sell his character and make the laughs play bigger. Edwards was pleased at his colleagues' approval of a difficult scene that he and Mitchum shot two days earlier on the veranda of The Breakers, arguably Newport's most famous cottage, in which he had to give Mitchum the pair of rubber underpants that would free him from his mansion prison.[1] Mitchum was playful during these scenes as well as phenomenally skilled. He raised or lowered his voice in perfect awareness of the camera's distance from his face and the focal length of the lens. He duplicated exactly his hand movements for each take (an editor's dream); and he underplayed his character's obvious amazement, if not shame, at such a forward act by the young North. At the end of one long take, he even ad-libbed to Edwards, "By the way, I just pissed myself" that brought down the audience at the dailies as it had the crew when he said it on the set.

"That'll be on the outtake reel for sure," someone said from the dark.

The lights went up after the dailies, allowing people to forage for Perrier, and a buzz shot through the room that Lauren Bacall had arrived, like royalty paying a State visit. She sat beside Virginia Madsen and sipped her bottled water.

"I found this wonderful video rental place here," she confided to Madsen while *The Dead* was being set up. "I rented *Grand Hotel* last night. Have you ever seen anything as exquisite as Garbo? She was the most perfect-looking woman. I met her once."

Madsen's eyes opened wide. "You did?"

"Yes. I was just leaving Cole Porter's house—and if *that* isn't enough name-dropping for you, I don't know what is—and she was coming in. She was wearing a sort of beige suit, her hair was the same color beige—and it was natural—and her skin was perfect, the same as a peach. I was nineteen and I was *very* impressed." (This, from one of the screen's other great beauties.)

Anjelica beckoned everyone back into the room to watch *The Dead*. It was a curious screening, one reel at a time on the rattling portable projector in the makeshift premiere theatre. It would not have its official opening until the end of the year. The sound was only passable, and the light leaked in from the street.

No matter. Nobody moved.

The Dead was adapted for the screen by John Huston and his older son Tony from the James Joyce novella that concludes his classic 1912 work (not published until 1914), *Dubliners*. Set in Dublin at the turn of the century, the action takes place at a dinner in a private home on the night of the Epiphany and soon focuses on the lives of Gretta and Ga-

---

1. Three of Newport's estates were edited together editorially to represent the single Bosworth house.

briel, a middle-aged couple who long ago settled into the mechanics of an unvarying marriage. On the night of a quiet snow, Gretta recalls, in her mind, a boy named Michael Furey, whom she loved and who loved her, and who died for his love, and the memory of this love haunts her soul. *The Dead* is one of the most beautifully written pieces in English literature, and the responsibility of translating it to motion pictures weighed heavily upon all who worked on it.

As the film concluded, Anjelica sat in anticipation of her peers' reaction.

It was not long in coming, and it was ecstatic. She later recalled of this evening, "You never know, when you're with friends, and you show your movie—unless there's a sort of terrible, stark silence afterward. Mercifully, I've never been privy to that kind of evening! But it was a very, very nice feeling.

"Actually, I loved seeing the film under those conditions, even though the color was off and the sound was bad. But there was something nice and gregarious in that room. I think it was my favorite showing. It was one of the better moments."

Many months later, she was able to talk, with some distance, about making *The Dead* and other films with her father. "Before I could walk, I had the impression that he commanded everything around him," she said, "and not by any effort of his own. I think he had the strongest presence of anyone I've met (this, from a woman who was famously involved with Jack Nicholson for over a decade), and it was extraordinary that a man who, towards the end of his life, was attached to oxygen tubes and confined mostly to a wheelchair, could still be the tallest and most powerful man in a room."[2]

Anjelica made her screen debut in her father's 1969 romantic movie, *A Walk With Love and Death*, although she had a tiny role in his *Sinful Davey* produced earlier that same year. Subsequent screen appearances were infrequent but impressive for the former model: *Gardens of Stone*, *Captain EO*, *The Last Tycoon*, *The Postman Always Rings Twice*, and even *Spinal Tap*. But she was best known for her work within the Huston family, a pedigree that seemed to make her untouchable by others. "I'm just not offered as many parts as I would like," she reported. "Or maybe it's just that I'm extremely selective— I can't quite figure out which. I think it's the same phenomenon I had when I was a model and was told, at age 15, that I was too sophisticated for the pages of *Glamour* magazine. So it's one of

---

2.   Subsequent interview with the Author on the film's formal release.

those things. It's maybe also that people haven't seen a lot of my work, and they mostly identify me with Maerose Prizzi." If they do, it is with good reason: not only did she make an impression in the 1985 black comedy about the husband-and-wife Mafia hit team, (opposite Jack Nicholson) she won an Oscar® for it.

If her demeanor seems secure, perhaps that is also acting. Truth be told, Anjelica Huston was not always as secure as she became, and it took an acting teacher to start her on the path to standing on her own.

"Peggy Furey was a most validating teacher," Anjelica stated. Furey was the first one who convinced her that she could act. "I think you're either born with it or you're not," she believed, "but someone who is insecure, as I was at a certain point, can be helped by going to acting class, and, particularly, by a teacher who is as reassuring as she was. I think there's a level of insecurity that's a constant, but I don't think it has any place in front of a camera unless that's what you're playing. I would say I'm a lot more secure now than I was before I went to Peggy, because I didn't know if I was any good or not."

Once she earned Furey's approval, she found her father "very inspirational to me. I could look at him and tell exactly what it was he wanted, and, if I was hard pressed to find something, I could look to him and find it."

Anjelica had another trick, a most personal one, which she drew upon while making *The Dead*. It was the similarity between the name of her acting teacher and Michael Furey, the boy who died showing his love for her character, Gretta.

"I think the last lines in the book are as close to immortal as you can get," she said. "There was very little about it that didn't strike home. I didn't know a Michael Furey, but I knew a Martin Furey and I knew a Peggy Furey. I knew those walks in the rain and I knew Galway and there was a lot to identify in it. I knew women like Gretta. There's that kind of style and the essence of that time that haven't gone out of Ireland; it still exists: gentility, decency, dignity and conversation, all of those things, and there are times that I miss radically. So there's very little that doesn't strike me about the book."

A woman's love for her father, an actress' love of her teacher, a character's love for another. Fact and fiction folded upon one another in *The Dead*, and among the people who made it. They carried this through to finishing *Mr. North*.

16

All Night Party

Gala parties have returned to the mansions of Newport, but it is only a movie. At The Elms, one of the grandest cottages on Bellevue Avenue, the makers of *Mr. North* hired an orchestra, outfitted the already grand ballroom with decorations, and invited dozens of formally attired couples to fill in the background. It was not for the entertainment of the participants, though, it was for the enjoyment of people who were not even there: the movie audience.

In the story, the opulent ball serves as background for the engagement announcement of Sarah (Sally) Boffin and Michael P. Ennis. Michael is the scion of a fabulously wealthy old-line family, and Sally, until recently, was the lowly house servant whom Mrs. Bailey-Lewis reprimanded in the first scene. When Virginia Madsen (Sarah/Sally) is presented to Mrs. Bailey-Lewis (Tammy Grimes), the haughty dowager's shocked swoon is to be one of the major laughs in the picture. (In the final version, instead of a swoon, Grimes's character goes into shock and mumbles the reprimand she once gave Sally.)

It takes a lot to throw a party that builds to a laugh, then tops it with a romance. Over the length of several warm August nights, the Elms was the focus of actors, crew, extras, caterers and, yes, authentic members of Newport's still-vital Society set who were invited to dance the night away, over and over again, as Danny Huston decreed. It was easy to tell the bluebloods from the professional extras; they were the ones who grumbled over being ordered about by assistant directors Tony Cerbone and Joe Brooks.

Between breeding and bleeding, all extras became equal when they gathered on the front steps of the great house hoping to snare a glimpse of the movie stars ensconced in the cordoned-off back lounge. Occasionally the two worlds mixed—an errant extra sneaked into the Hollywood sanctum—but he or she would be swiftly ejected by Dan Ferreira. Ferreira owned the North Dartmouth, Massachusetts limousine fleet who not only saw that the stars got where they belonged, but also that they were left alone once they got there. Gruff but lovable, Ferreira earned the respect of everyone by treating all comers, stellar or cellar, as equals. One interloper who momentarily sneaked past the able Ferreira was a film editor from a local TV station seeking a souvenir. Her target: a handwritten sign imploring "No cameras, please." Her mission failed.

Then there was the fabled mother-daughter autograph hounds from Boston who sneaked around the garden side of The Elms, past security guards, hoping to spot a star. Harmless but persistent, they nearly got more than they bargained for when Anthony Edwards, desperate to beat the long lavatory lines, sneaked into the darkness of the garden to relieve himself over the edge of a railing. Fortunately, the autograph hunters had left by then. Good thing this was decades before cell phone cameras. Nevertheless, regular cameras proved to be the common denominator between "society" and "rabble." As the long sessions progressed, the scene was expected to take half a week of grueling night shoots, and it became normal during breaks to have snapshot cameras whipped out of period handbags, aimed furtively toward Mitchum and other others, flash, and be restored to their bejeweled hiding places.

The crew call was routinely 6 P.M. at The Elms and carried through to dawn. Somebody forgot to make adequate catering arrangements for the hundred or so extras, and most felt inconvenienced on the first night; reparations were made subsequently.

Huston and Vidgeon methodically compiled their latticework of shots, some wide to show off the splendor of the mirrored ballroom, and others intimate to highlight the tender reunion of Sally (Madsen) and North (Edwards). In the story, it was his counsel that enabled her to land the handsome and dashing Ennis. With the need to get as many set-ups (shots) as quickly as possible, repositioning the camera and lights can waste an hour, the camera was mounted on a dolly. This decision not only gave a sweep to the shots themselves, but allowed it to glide freely on the smooth marble floors. Choreographing the camera through the swirling extras became the job of a traffic cop more than an assistant director, ably assisted by the team of grips.

There were further delays when actress Madsen refused to be photographed unless her hair had been arranged by her personal hairdresser.

He could not be found and production stopped for an hour while he was located.

Then the TV news crews showed up.

Joel Siegel, film critic for ABC-TV's *Good Morning America*, arrived with his producer and camera crew to get a story and, not incidentally, generate important production publicity that would increase the film's commercial profile. Siegel, perky and mustachioed, grew increasingly impatient with the cast and crew who, for reasons that seemed to escape him, were more concerned with making their movie than talking to him. After hours of having to keep out of their way, Siegel's producer shouted, "Would everybody please be quiet? We're trying to make a television program!"

That became the cast and crew's first real joke of the night. As the punch line, the diminutive Siegel did not laugh.

By the wee hours, the actors, most of whom had been waiting around since early evening, began trying to grab a few moments' sleep in their lounge. Some did embroidery (Grimes) or read (Bacall) or just sat together and ignored everyone else (Mitchum and Harry Dean Stanton). Mitchum, in particular, was becoming edgy. He was due to return to *War and Remembrance* once this sequence wrapped and he was worried that it might spill over into another day.

While Madsen (her hair freshly coiffed) and Edwards were called in front of the cameras for their dramatic scene, Madsen's screen "husband" was talking with Lauren Bacall. In a normal world, an actor hired for one day's work would not mix with a star of Bacall's stature. But the young man playing Michael P. Ennis was not just any actor. He was Christopher Lawford, the thirty-ish son of Peter Lawford and Patricia Kennedy (of *the* Kennedys). Young Lawford was a former model who was starting to devote his energies to developing as an actor.

"That's my surrogate mother over there," the Lawford scion said, nodding toward Bacall. "We've known each other—"

"Just a minute!" Bacall shot back with perfect timing. Had the two been sharing stories from their colorful pasts? "Don't tell him anything!" she barked. She wasn't joking; behind her tough-sounding language lurked an even tougher resolve.

"Not a thing," Lawford promised. "My lips are sealed."

"Remember! He's a reporter!" Bacall warned, and returned to her reading. But she hovered within hearing range, ready to interrupt at the drop of a famous name. Despite this, Lawford relaxed and, with the grace of his lineage, talked about his character.

"Michael Ennis is an aristocratic Bostonian who married the maid," he said crisply. "What can I tell you? High visibility, not a lot of lines. I get the girl. That's the key consideration. [As for] the acting career right now"—he nodded toward his agent, Ann Dollard, who had come from Los Angeles to visit—"we're concentrating on anything we can get. I'll dance at Bar Mitzvahs."

Not surprisingly, Lawford grew up knowing that he would have a wide choice of careers. It took him a while to find his direction. "I went to law school to get off the street and stay out of trouble," he said, only half-joking. "It was, for my contemporaries, just a natural progression. I graduated [Boston College] Law School about three years ago and just never got into it; I don't know that many of my contemporaries who are practicing law who are real happy. That's an indication to me that it's something I would not want to go into. So I tried some other stuff for a while."

The other "stuff" was acting.

"A lot of people say the two aren't entirely dissimilar," Lawford averred. "But as far as I can see, they're light years apart."

Having grown up in the public eye and feeling the heat thrown off by his famous family, Lawford realized that he was being handed opportunities for which he might not have been prepared. "So I spend a lot of time in New York and I plan to spend a lot of time in L.A. this year to get some work. I just signed with Leading Artists, (Dollard perked up at the mention) so it's growing. I'd like to start doing some theatre, because I have virtually no training and I'm interested in doing this well.

"Most people, when I walk in the door of the casting director or the director or the producer, assume, because of my father, that I've been doing this for a long period of time. But I came into this business late, so there's that misconception to deal with. But, on the other hand, I get in to see a lot of people because of who I am, which probably wouldn't happen if I wasn't. So they balance each other."

His attention was immediately drawn to Bacall, who pretended not to be listening. "Look around," he said, gazing around the room at the dramatis personae. "It's like a slumber party. A formal slumber party. People playing dress-up. It's kind of fun, but it's also tedious. You wait around a lot, but where can you wait around with all these people, drink coffee, and wear black tie? I'm thirty-two going on twelve. I suppose you could call all actors young-at-heart or child-like. It seems to me that, in order to make something good, it has to be spontaneous, full of wonder—all of those things that children have, and that we as grownups spend our lives losing. That aspect of it is certainly attractive to me."

Did he feel that he was becoming a good actor? Before he could answer, Bacall interrupted. "What are you doing to that kid?" she demanded, "Don't answer that! Tell him to find out!"

"You'll find out when you see the film," Lawford backtracked, adding a wink. "I'm being taught. I'm watching these great people around here at work."

"Watching us sit around." Bacall huffed in her famous, throaty, New York-tinged and, by now, humorless voice.

At about this time, another presence was making itself known on the set. He was a tall, dark man walking slowly around on long legs, and he was carrying a volume of the complete works of Eugene O'Neill. He was not dressed to appear in the film, yet none of the security personnel asked him to leave. When he found Anjelica Huston and approached her, his identity was confirmed. This was Tony Huston, Anjelica's brother, Danny's half-brother, and the man who adapted James Joyce's *The Dead* for their father to direct.

A local newspaper had run a story that the President (Ronald Reagan at the time) had tried phoning Huston at the hospital, but the doctors refused to let the call through. This was not the subject of Tony's and Anjelica's conversation (actors are always trying to get to speak to directors). Anjelica was more anxious about press reports that painted her father's condition as being graver than the hospital was admitting. She had gone so far as to release a statement to the contrary through the producers and was eager to break silence to discuss his status.

"He seems very much an inspiration to people, particularly people who are not particularly well," Anjelica offered. "He's tremendously courageous. He doesn't let go of life. He's had plenty of opportunity [to let go] and he's constantly interested, and an extremely vital man." She acknowledged that legends surrounded her father, both true and false. "If it's a good story, it's a good story," she joked pragmatically. "He's been on many adventures." Her liquid eyes glowed with admiration and intelligence. "He *relishes* adventure! I think it's a fine line between what you fear and what makes your heart beat faster, and I think he's certainly been a man who's gone for the rush of adrenaline in his time. He likes wild places and wild situations. I think his movies reflect that; his general interest isn't locked into one particular thing. He can go into the Congo, he can find it in Ireland, he can find it in Mexico, whatever it is that excited him. He has this extraordinary ability to translate his excitement, and what it is that inspires him, to film."

Tony stepped onto the porch of The Elms, O'Neill still in hand, and breathed deeply of the Newport air before explaining why he was toting around this literary talisman. "I find it tonic," he said in a clipped, partly British accent that belied his birth in Malibu, California thirty-seven years earlier. "There are writers whom you read when you're trying to write something and they make you feel sick because it seems to all come so easily to them. Well, O'Neill is someone quite different. O'Neill is someone who is struggling to express; he's got tremendous guts. Even if he can't quite make it, it's an heroic struggle to try and wrest sense out of prose. A very, very good writer to read if you're also trying to make dramatic sense. Great balls."

How did *The Dead* come about, and how did Huston *fils* become involved? "I just recently heard that Dad first thought of *The Dead* as a viable project back when he was making *Moby Dick* (1956), which was the first film set I ever went on. I remember when I was seventeen or eighteen, and I was enamored of Joyce and *Dubliners* in particular, talking about *The Dead* which is, of course, the outstanding story in that collection, and asking him about making it into a film, and even talking with people we knew and how they might have played various characters."

The project eventually came together while John was directing *Under the Volcano* in 1984, financed by two producers who would later produce *The Dead*. "They were talking about how few films existed which actually discuss the interior life of marriage," Tony recalled. "There were lots of films which were about the breakups or falling in love or that side, but relatively little that had to do with what actually went on when two people were committed to one another. And somehow *The Dead* came up.

"Anyway," the precise Tony said impatiently, "they got the rights and I was in London with Dad when Dad was doing his first picture with Danny, *Mr. Corbett's Ghost*. And [producer] Ray Stark had asked Dad to give some advice about a project Ray Stark had been offered. Dad always collaborates with somebody, and he didn't have anybody on hand at that time, and he said, 'Tony, how'd you like to collaborate with me?' knowing that I was a struggling writer. I'd written a few screenplays and things, so Dad and I began to collaborate, and out of that relationship, which was the first time I'd ever worked with Dad as an adult, he felt sufficiently confident of me that when *The Dead* came up, he was able to suggest that I write the screenplay. It's been the greatest pleasure of my adult life, without any doubt, that I now have a marvelous working relationship with

Dad. I'm now involved in the third screenplay—we've also done a treatment or two—which we worked on together, and it's been great."

If the elder Huston was known for tackling such literary giants as Melville, Kipling, Hemingway, and Forster, the younger Huston is no less ambitious. "The project that I'm working on at the moment is based on the famous duel between Alexander Hamilton and Aaron Burr. HBO has commissioned it, and I'm hoping, and I believe, it will be a feature film. It's the most marvelous story, and there's the possibility of doing something quite unique. You have these wonderful Eighteenth Century people who know how to express themselves beyond a grunt and a groan."

Huston became studious as he recounted this misunderstood moment of American history. "Everybody knows about Hamilton and Burr and that they fought a duel, but beyond that they're kind of vague. So it's actually a very fertile thing. It's something that is in the American subconscious: there's Alexander Hamilton on the ten dollar bill."[1]

It was nearing dawn as the cast and crew wrapped for the day and Tony joined Anjelica, Alegra, and Danny for another trip to visit their father at the hospital. Having all four children in town might give John joy, but it also looked ominous. The reports from the hospital offered little in the way of new information, even for those few whose status allowed them to cut through the noncommittal cover story.

---

1. The picture was never made.

17

Speaking of Huston

John Huston may have been absent from the set of *Mr. North*, but his presence was as tangible as the lavish locations where the movie was being made. This was no accident: the key production people were either his selection, had worked with him in the past, or were so moved by his screen work that they carried a touch of the Huston spark even when he was not physically present. Like the Newport mansions, the 81-year-old Huston was an enduring symbol of a time when values were different. Unlike the stone buildings, however, Huston was very much alive, and everyone had a favorite story about him.

Anjelica Huston: "He stirs a lot of emotions in me that are very useful. As a director he's very available to actors, and I use it to my advantage."

Lauren Bacall: "Bogie (Humphrey Bogart, her late husband) always said that, if there's an impossible location, you can be sure John will find it. John's authentic. He wants to shoot a movie where it takes place. And when John is making a movie, he doesn't care what is going on in the world. The two films where I've been on location with them, *The Treasure of the Sierra Madre* in Mexico and *The African Queen* in Africa, are two physically uncomfortable locations, and I was in charge of organizing lunch for the company. In Africa, I used to go on the boat up the river in the Congo bringing the lunch. I made [the native servants] wipe every plate. In Africa, you know, they don't like taking orders from women. I was a bit nervous at times."

Producer Skip Steloff recalled wanting script changes and discussing with his partners how to go about asking for them. "We'd been rehearsing it in the car for two hours. We said what we had to say and he listened to everyone. When it was all done, he went one by one to each of us and asked, 'Okay, what are *your* credentials, lad?' And this is with the oxygen tank hanging down. He moved right down the line of us: 'What are *your* credentials, lad?" "What are *your* credentials, lad?' When he gets to me, I say, 'I'm a buccaneer, just like you, and I've come to finance your picture.' He lets out a laugh. 'Atta boy,' he said. 'Let's go.'"

Tammy Grimes: "When we were rehearsing (with John present), Danny was very quiet. He would ask one question or say one thing and John would nod yes or no. And you could tell by his facial expression whether he was pleased, or what he was thinking. John would say, 'Don't you think he's going on a bit?' or 'Don't you think we should have to cut that?' And Danny would say, 'Oh, no, no, no' and John would say, "For you, I'll keep it in.'"

Janet Roach: "There's one line in *Prizzi's Honor*: 'I didn't get married so my wife could keep working.' John never understood that that line was funny because he thinks women *shouldn't* work when they're married, or something. He gives me the gig about being a feminist. And I give him the gig about being a few things!"

Lauren Bacall: Bogie was in the cast (of *Key Largo*, which Huston made in 1948), as was Lionel Barrymore, Claire Trevor—not bad actors, you know—and myself. I was paying attention to John and I was thrilled, *thrilled* to work with him. There was a scene in which Eddie Robinson was [verbally] attacking Franklin Roosevelt, and Lionel Barrymore had to defend him. Well, Lionel Barrymore—whom I adored—*hated* Roosevelt. And most of us, of course, loved him. Lionel had to defend Roosevelt so strongly that he had to get up—he was in a wheelchair then—he had to get up out of the wheelchair and go after Robinson, and then fall. John loved to watch his face when he had to say that Roosevelt was a great man! John enjoyed situations like that. You see, John instills great trust, which is the best way to direct. He has a great gift for that, and when you trust your director, you feel you're able to try anything, because you know he will always stop you when you've gone too far. With some directors you find you have to protect yourself but, with John, you're willing to take chances because you know he won't allow you to make any more of a fool of yourself than we all do every day."

18

Child's Play

Robert Mitchum departed as discretely as he had come. After three weeks of substituting for the still-hospitalized Huston, Mitchum finished his scenes, dropped by The Elms with a bottle of Courvoisier to toast his compatriots, and left.

"He's keeping up the old tradition," cracked a crew member who added that he was not sorry to see the ill-tempered actor go. "Get the hell out of town before they find something else for you to do."

But the crew was looking forward to three more weeks' work, nearly all of it involving Anthony Edwards, who had, by then, become a charmed presence and respected colleague. Edwards appeared in practically every scene and, in the role, had to maintain a balance between wide-eyed optimism and intelligent pragmatism. In other words, Theophilus North is nobody's fool, but he is not glib about it. The challenge invigorated the young actor, who was tackling his first starring role.

"It's rare in a movie to have a scene between two people that's seven or eight pages long," he noted, and he was right: most modern films, catering to a perception of an audience's short attention span, change scenes every three or four pages. "It's rare, but it's a luxury. But that's Thornton Wilder. It's all in the script if you know where to look for it. When you do a period piece, the dialogue and its style become a part of it. And also a style of lighting and dress and walking. The rhythm comes from the dialogue and the way you speak it. When a script is written correctly, it comes out of the dialogue."

That was not the normal talk one expected to hear from a young Hollywood actor. When he made *Mr. North*, Anthony "Tony" Edwards was on the cusp of stardom. He had a "nice guy" image that later played out on the hit television series, *E.R.*, even as George Clooney and Maria Bello were the ones whose stars took off from that show.

The Santa Barbara, California-born Edwards was encouraged to enter acting by his parents, who were not actors, but who sent him to London while he was still a teenager to start his education in stagecraft. Returning to the States to finish his education, he took acting at the University of Southern California but chose not to complete his courses when Hollywood lights shone. His first noticeable appearance was in *Heart Like a Wheel*, then *Gotcha*, and the surprise hit, *Revenge of the Nerds*. He was John Cusack's conspiratorial friend in *The Sure Thing*, and landed *Mr. North* after beating out (according to the producers) higher profile young actors like Rob Lowe. What drew attention to Edwards' abilities was his role as "Goose," Tom Cruise's best friend in the blockbuster war film, *Top Gun*. "Goose" was the proverbial "comical sidekick" and, in Hollywood formula filmmaking, that meant only one thing.

"He had *dead man* written on his forehead." Edwards could afford to joke about the job that opened the door to stardom. "I liked the way the role was written, but I also knew it was going to be one of those heartbreaker roles—a great guy who dies. 'Let's get the guy with the wife and kid!' He had humor, a perspective on the Navy, he was all set up to do it right. He wasn't a Commie-killer—well, it doesn't really matter whether he was or not.

"After *Top Gun* I took a year off and didn't do anything but theatre, which is really what I grew up doing. From the time I was twelve till I was seventeen, I did theatre—thirty plays before I got out of high school. It was like being in Little League baseball. There's a group called the Santa Barbara Youth Theatre which puts together professional, pro-am shows where they bring professionals up from L.A. and the kids get to work with them."

When he got the lead in *Mr. North*, he realized he was its center, but not its focus. "It *is* called *Mr. North*, but I don't feel any pressure. There are great people here and a lot of support. Everybody's here to make a good movie. The pressure is when you have no dialogue to work with; the pressure's on when you have to make really bad material work. *That's* pressure.

"You make a lot of movies—some of 'em you're proud of and some of 'em you're not. And some of 'em nobody sees. For a lot of people, *Top Gun* was the only movie I was ever in. You can't change it; that's the only movie they saw, because that movie was successful. But if you look at an actor, any actor, you're surprised at how many movies they make. I did a television series with Richard Crenna (*It Takes Two*, 1982-1983) and he gave me great advice. He said sometimes you have to make a movie because you like the location, because every movie's *supposed* to be good and every movie is *meant* to be good, and some obviously have better scripts than others, but if it's a toss-up between the two, go with the location because you're going to make a hundred movies and some of them are gonna be good and some of 'em are gonna be bad and you don't have any control over that. You're an actor. In that way, you can't say that because I was in *Top Gun* it was a hit movie." Then Edwards grinned, "But you also can't say, if *Top Gun* had failed, that it was my fault. If a movie makes $200 million, no matter how bad it was, very few people will say it's a bad movie. But if it *doesn't* make any money, bingo, it's a bad movie." He shakes his head and sighs. "Good and bad movies are so personal."

Edwards was the youngest of five children in a family that goes back four Southern California generations. Many of his relatives were designers, a profession he traces to his grandfather on his mother's side, who was an Art Deco artist in the 1930s. "He designed the Disney studios and also worked with Cecil B. DeMille as a conceptual artist in Hollywood. He died the year that I was born. My mother lived in Hollywood and then moved out to Santa Barbara later, in high school. She met my dad up there; he came over before World War I to design exhibition at the San Francisco World's Fair and the war broke out and he couldn't go home. It's amazing how that works out."

Edwards had a lot of time to consider such things since arriving in Newport over the July 4 weekend. Far from his friends, far from Hollywood, he explored the town between rehearsals and tried to settle into a non-L.A. way of living. One difference between east and west stuck in his mind.

"Slowest drivers in the world," he said of Newport. "But very polite. Everybody lets other people in. In L.A., we just shoot people on the freeway: if they're going too fast or too slow, they just get shot. I was listening to Boston morning radio talking about L.A.—let's face it, Boston is not the drivers education capitol of the world."

Speaking of education, the subject returns to Theophilus North and his optimistic quest for Truth. Both disciplines inspired Edwards.

"If there's any point to this movie, it's Truth. That's what's so great about this character. Be honest, be truthful, be strong, understand—don't accept stupidity or ignorance. Be optimistic because you're smart, not because you're stupid."

It was Edwards' ability to portray Theophilus North's optimism without detaching him from reality that endeared him to Huston and landed him the job. Talking with the actor, one quickly realizes that his optimism is genuine. "I don't know if Man is necessarily getting worse," he offered. "He's getting better. If we're *not* getting better, what's the point? What's the point if we're just here to do time?"

North's optimism in the story is not restricted to his Scripture readings for John McHenry Bosworth. He also displays it as a tutor for a gaggle of moppets in a scene shot in the Tennis Hall of Fame at the fringe of Millionaires' Row. The child actors were dressed in spotless white duds for the occasion, and, off screen as well as on, Edwards acted as their cheerleader, prancing ahead of them along the chalked lines like a human version of *Make Way for Ducklings*. Along with the children, aged five to twelve, came their mothers, aged somewhat higher. Assistant director Joe Brooks, who, when he used to be an actor, portrayed the rotund, nearsighted Fort Courage lookout on TV's *F Troop*, gathered the kids in front of him and handed out official-looking release forms.

"My name's Joe Brooks," he told the cherubs. "Tell your Mommy to fill out one of these." While the kids carried out Brooks' orders, Robin Vidgeon took out a snapshot camera and grabbed some photos of the little dears. Danny Huston remained businesslike with the kids, lining them up and making sure that they all knew each other (in the story, they are all friends). Soon the kids' mothers joined the snapshot-shooting brigade.

Along the perimeter of the superlatively groomed tennis court, Frank Keever's crew was finishing the task of making the 1987 location look like it had in 1926. Not surprisingly, it didn't have that far to go; little had changed in 61 years, and that which had was soon disguised behind lace curtains (hiding modern building interiors), freezing the large roof clock at 1:50, shutting down a noisy ventilating system, and ensuring that the main doors stay closed so as not to reveal the modern shopping center across the street. The crew worked fast to accommodate the child actors' short attention spans. They also had to work fast to capture the wide shots before the sun moved across the sky, casting building shadows that would be difficult to match in editing. That was just one of Vidgeon's concerns.

Vidgeon came to his position as Director of Photography after 27 years assisting Douglas Slocombe, the famed British cinematographer of such acclaimed and photographically diverse films as *Raiders of the Lost Ark*, *Jesus Christ Superstar*, and *The Great Gatsby*, which first brought him to Newport, and these same locations, in 1974. On his own for *Mr. North*, Vidgeon was trying some unusual touches.

"Almost the whole of this movie, I've shot through a very fine gauze over the lens," the blush-faced, bearded craftsman described with his British penchant for precision. "When Anthony and the kids are at the tennis court, you've got brilliant sunlight, green grass, and they're all in whites, so the gauze over the lens makes the costumes flare very slightly. In my eyes and in Danny's eye, it adds to the feeling of heat."

Vidgeon found that the opulence of Newport added value to the visuals. "Because of the mansions, even when we're going close-up, we use wide-angle lenses so that the background stays sharp. I've always had a feeling that it seems a terrible pity to pay for a really good art director such as Eugene Lee and then shoot half the stuff on long lenses so the focus falls off six inches behind the artist and you can't see the set." On the other hand, wide angle lenses are not flattering to actors. Vidgeon kept this in mind.

"Apart from Lauren Bacall and Anjelica Huston, where we've done glamour-type close-ups, most close-ups have been with wide lenses." He and Bacall "had a discussion before she started. She's very aware [that] it's not 40 years ago." He smiled diplomatically, confessing, "I'm older than I was 40 years ago."

Prior to *Mr. North*, Vidgeon shot *Mr. Corbett's Ghost* for Danny Huston, and then Clive Barker's breakthrough feature film, *Hellraiser*. Mindful that some of his work was intended for theatres and some for television, he said of his craft, "It doesn't matter where the image ends up. Whether you put it onto a satellite and beam it up to Borneo or onto a movie screen, you put the same amount of care. But *this* story," he said proudly, "is being made for theatres."

Back on the set, Joe Brooks and Anthony Edwards were rehearsing the children.

"Don't laugh at the funny parts," Brooks tells them. "It spoils the scene." His patience was tested, but whenever the kids started to get too unruly, he squinted like he used to do as Trooper Vanderbilt on *F Troop* and the peanut gallery squealed in delightful recognition. "Thank God for reruns," he sighed.

By the time the crew wrapped for the day, their spirits were bolstered. Word reached the set that John Huston had been released from the hospital after twenty-two days in intensive care. He is expected to visit the set before the end of the week, even if only to greet old friends from the back of his car. It was Wednesday, August 19, and the good news midway through production, which was courting exhaustion and ennui, is just what everybody needed. It must be true, people were saying, because production supervisor Ann Shaw, days away from delivering her child, was expected to close the production office and join her father, Tommy, on location. She would not do that if Huston wasn't going to be there.

19

False Alarm

Huston did not show on Friday as hoped, nor on Saturday, nor was there any word from Sea Meadow, his rented house, to which he was discharged from hospital. If anything, Maricela was more discrete than Charlton Memorial Hospital in protecting Huston from inquiries. Her sole concern was his health and safety.

The drought of information generated colorful, if hopeful, rumors. The chief one was that the hospital I.C.U. did not really release Huston; he used his Irish charm to persuade the medical staff that he was well enough to leave. Be it truth or wishful thinking, it showed that people wanted the legend to continue.

Huston or no, his company was hard at work keeping the film on its relentless schedule. They moved to the waterfront vista of Washington Street, near a small public park, and a row of large, wooden, private homes. It sounds like some Yuppie-infested reclaimed cobblestone waterfront, but it wasn't. This was where normal people lived.

The company borrowed a Victorian wood home and then tarpaulined off its living room to block the sun and make interior shots appear to be filmed at night. It looked almost as if it was tented for termite extermination, but this was for actors. The trick was simple but it enabled the crew and cast to keep normal hours and avoid the overtime expense of night shift. The inside of the cramped home was turned into Mrs. Cranston's boarding house. Newport's Finest controlled passing traffic; the location was three blocks from the Navy's War College.

In Wilder's novel, Mrs. Cranston is proprietor of what amounts to a retirement home for ex-servants. These can be people who were in service in the great cottages and retired, or became too infirm to continue their duties, or who were "let go" for other reasons. In the days before pension plans, IRAs, and Social Security, and if their employers hadn't made proper arrangements, they faced their declining years with little more than memories unless someone like Mrs. Cranston took them in.

Lauren Bacall and Harry Dean Stanton waited weeks to perform their primary scenes. They played Newport's most esteemed servants: she a retired housekeeper, he the "Governor" of the town's butlers and footmen. They represent the flip side of the bluebloods, who consider the community to be theirs alone. Because Theophilus North is allowed to enter the mansions through the front doors, he is not permitted to take rooms in Mrs. Cranston's house; nevertheless, he is welcome to call on its residents. This evening, in the story, North is asked to minister to one of Mrs. Cranston's older residents. Although the summer night is full of life, he is asked to ease this elderly woman to her imminent death. Tanni has seen three generations of other people's families grow from infancy to maturity, and each, in turn, has left her behind. Now she dies alone and forgotten, tormented by promises unfulfilled and the painful abandonment at the ungrateful hands of those she cared for all her life. In order to give closure, Mrs. Cranston has sent for Mr. North.

It is a scene which Huston and Roach had cut from the shooting script, but that they later reinstated. The reasons vary. One faction insisted that, without it, the already lean script might wind up under its contracted 90-minute running time.[1] Another said that the production was far enough under budget to allow the scene to be shot. Either excuse made sense, and the actors, especially Harriet Rogers, a popular Boston stage and television actress cast as the nanny, was thrilled to shoot the "restored" sequence. Ken Reiner, a production executive who joined the company on location, explained how Rogers landed the role.

"It was one of the more human, heartwarming moments in the script, but it had to go" he said. "Then when we decided to restore the scene, we called to see actresses, and Harriet was one who showed up. She must weigh eighty pounds dripping wet, but she has a wonderful spirit that made her just right for the scene, which just holds your heart in its hands. We've been very lucky to have some very good people aboard this show."

The Cranston location was hot and was as shut off from fresh air as was the courthouse the week before. Because the scene was so intimate, only minimal crew were allowed inside, and the rest lounged around on the weedy front lawn reading papers, catching sun, or chewing the fat.

1.　The completed film runs 89 minutes. A squeaker.

One man who would look in keeping with any of the crew members, but is, in fact, one of the stars, was Harry Dean Stanton. Stanton sat cross-legged behind a row of bushes, just inside the house's driveway, shirt off, trying to maintain his tan. Stanton, a familiar face in dozens of movies, never thought of himself as a screen archetype, yet the busy sixty-year-old character actor found himself among the ranks of Gary Cooper, Ben Johnson, Henry Fonda, James Stewart, John Wayne, and Spencer Tracy as men whose presence in a film served as short-hand for "American."

"That's complimentary, if anything," the weathered Stanton accepted in his soft drawl. "I never planned on it. It was just there instinctively, unconsciously." And it had been there through thirty years of screen work in such notable titles as *The Missouri Breaks, Wise Blood* (for Huston), *Straight Time* and countless others. His greatest fame may accrue from the 1984 *Repo Man*, which defies description except that it stars Emilio Estevez as a car repossessor who repossesses more than cars. It was Stanton's offbeat performance as Estevez's co-star that made the younger film generation embrace him, although he bristled at the "cult" designation.

"The young people are avant-garde, and the avant-garde is open-minded," he said. "I like to think of myself as being fairly aware of what's going on in the world, and so-called 'cult' movies are the same way. *Repo Man* is not just a cult movie, it's visionary. It's a satire on a whole state of affairs. It's the desperation of a man looking for a job, living under the threat of nuclear annihilation. It satirizes religion, which obviously is not working today; it's corrupt and has been for centuries, as far as I'm concerned. The point being, it's not just a cult film, it's very aware and visionary. There's always a connotation to the word *cult* that's not necessarily a positive image."

Stanton also rejected the mindless action films that have since come to dominate Hollywood production but were, as he spoke in 1987, just starting to take hold. "There's never been a lot of good material going around, but it's been worse the last few years. The whole world seems to be going through a cataclysmic upheaval. It's more than escapism; it's just grossness and total insensitivity and violence and sickness. If you're a performing artist of any kind—actor, dancer, basketball player—you're an influence and, once you are, it's a big responsibility to make sure you have a positive influence without preaching or being boring. As actors, we should be able to play a totally evil person totally, and have you understand or identify with the evil, like the Chinese *yin-yang*. They accept evil as part of life. That doesn't mean that they *like* evil, but they accept that it exists."

As Stanton sunned himself he did a crossword puzzle. A car pulled up and Mary Stuart Masterson got out. Masterson had been away for a few days but returned to finish her small role as Elspeth Skeel, a teenager prone to migraine headaches which Mr. North cures with his celebrated static charge. She immediately joined Stanton.

"You know what you should include," said the young star of *Some Kind of Wonderful*, talking about Stanton. "How fast he fills in a crossword puzzle. In ink. And he's never wrong." It is true; Stanton was whizzing through the *New York Times* puzzle as if he already knew the answers. The two immediately fell into conversation. "I've quit drinking and smoking," she announced, "so we'll have nothing to do, nothing to talk about."

Masterson sprawled her tiny frame on the lawn and propped her chin on her wrists. "I think it's so neat, the magical elements in the script that are constantly denied, but they're present, whether it be magic from without, an external magic, or an internal magic. It's there, some force that's sort of placed on these people that Mr. North touches, or it's within the people who get healed by him. I think it's really neat that John Huston would be so attracted to that, now in his life."

"The indefinable things in life," Stanton interjected. "Magic, spirit, or Nirvana. Somebody, everybody wants to follow, sometimes blindly."

"They don't ask questions."

"They're looking for somebody else to have them instead of saving themselves."

But attention can disappear, as people in Hollywood learn. Masterson recalled the wisdom of writer Horton Foote (*A Trip to Bountiful, Tender Mercies*): "He said that money is such an ephemeral thing: one day you make a million dollars on a movie and you have the pseudo-respect of the people paying you the money. And if it doesn't do well, the next time around, you don't get paid and the movie doesn't get made. But if, the first time around, you make a good movie, then the second time around you'll get a shot at making another good movie, whether the first has made money or not."

Sometimes a movie is not completely good, though it has good pieces, Stanton offered: "You always go for moments, especially when you're first starting out. When I started out I did television and I knew that most of it was crap. I just tried to get a true moment here and there. You just try to relate honestly with people, and, hopefully, you'll wind up being sincere."

Masterson is the daughter of Peter Masterson, who directed the film version of *A Trip to Bountiful*, a moving tale of a woman revisiting her birthplace in preparation for dying. Geraldine Page's performance in the film won her an Oscar®. Until now, Stanton had not made the connection between daughter and father.

"I didn't know your father directed *A Trip to Bountiful*," he said.

"Did you know Geraldine?" asked Masterson.

Stanton looked down at his crossword puzzle and said evenly, "I went with her for a year and a half."

Masterson remained equally pokerfaced. "That's long enough."

20

Budget Sundays

Tammy Grimes was parking her car, not an easy maneuver, considering how laden it was with all the objects she had managed to collect in the few weeks she was in Newport. She insisted on residing in a second-floor room at the Budget Motor Inn overlooking the parking lot. It seems that that was where the motel's sole shade tree was growing, and it broke the sun-drenched monotony of her roadside vista. Having finished her scenes, Grimes was slated to return to New York City if she could stuff her possessions into the yellow Chevette which she affectionately called "the bumblebee." Over the previous six weeks, the legendary Broadway star had been quite the Bohemian. She dabbled in acrylic painting, glued glass chips and feathers into impromptu designs, and artfully cluttered her room with enough knickknacks to earn it the name "Tammy's Garage Sale" from co-workers who helped her add to it.

The husky-voiced, Tony®-winning star was born in Lynn, Massachusetts, not far from Boston, and became the toast of New York in 1960 as *The Unsinkable Molly Brown* as well as America's leading interpreter of Noel Coward. In real life, Grimes was no stranger to the aristocratic lifestyle into which she was cast in *Mr. North*. She was raised amid such plush Boston settings as the Chestnut Hill Country Club, Beaver Country Day School, and Stephens Junior College. High Society, therefore, was not unknown to her.

"One either is an aristocrat or one is not," Grimes noted objectively. "It has to do with the manner of a person, the way you were brought up. Once a lady, always a lady," she announced primly, then arched her eyebrows for effect, "depending on the definition of what a lady is."

Grimes was very much the lady, as well as an actress, a combination that non-actors have been known to refute. "You always feel a bit of an outsider," she confirmed, "but, then, you tend to get away with things, too. When you dine at the country club—very stuffy!—or go to the golf club for lunch, you don't have to wear the white pants and sweater and white shirt. You can kind of go as you are; you're the Bohemian eccentric that's been invited by the gentry."

She credited her father with giving her a sense of drama and, after finishing *Mr. North*, was looking forward to being his neighbor at an artists' colony she was forming in New Hampshire. "I've bought land. It's called the House of Pamplemousse, which is the name of my cat. The Pamplemousse Art Colony is going to be a series of little houses where you can work. My father lives not far away, so he'll be an inspiration to all of us, with stories you can't believe."

One of the Pamplemousse features would be a huge stone wall which Grimes planned to construct out of the rocks she collects during her travels. "That must weigh 300 pounds," she said, pointing to a wooden strongbox containing the personally selected stones that dominated her room at the Budget Motor Inn.

"My father says about the Budget, 'I think it's a very unlikely title for you, but probably very healthy. I keep getting your letters on Ritz-Carlton stationery with the address on the envelope as the Budget Motor Inn. There's an incongruity there.'"

And so there was an incongruity to Tammy Grimes. At once regal and fluttery, serene and spontaneous, the ingénue and the sophisticate, she threw off an air of unpredictability that had been first noticed by none other than Noel Coward, who "discovered" her for Broadway. "I was singing in a little cabaret called Upstairs at the Downstairs in New York City," she said while sitting in the middle of the Budget's orange bedspread, sipping grapefruit juice from the mouth of an inelegant jar. "He (Coward) was doing a play called *Look After Lulu*, which was based on a Feydeau farce, and Roddy McDowall, who is a great chum, said, 'Noel, I've got your Lulu but you've got to go and see her perform.'" This was in 1959. "He got Noel over. I was aware of the fact that he was there, of course, and shook like a leaf for twenty-two minutes. I didn't sing *one* Noel Coward song, which also made me shake even more. When I got through, he offered me the part of Lulu."

Look After Lulu didn't hit, but Grimes did, and brought her power to Meredith Willson's musical *The Unsinkable Molly Brown*, keeping it afloat through sheer stage presence despite the show's near-scuttling by the critics. Ironically, because she was not yet a big enough star to win her name above the title, she was forced into the "Supporting Actress" category come Tony time, even though, by any other definition, she was the lead.

A marriage to actor Christopher Plummer brought the couple a daughter, Amanda Plummer, who also became an acclaimed actress.

Whether saving a show or collecting rocks, Grimes' credo was that an actor's first responsibility is to keep from being boring.

"Actors will tell the same stories, but they'll refine them. It's like a fish tale [where] the fish gets bigger and bigger. They'll embellish, and they'll do it on purpose to see how the listener reacts. It isn't like writers who, when they tell a story, are really writing a book. Actors do it for a different reason: to entertain. When I go to the theatre now, I see it. I saw it in [Lanford Wilson's play] *Fences* and, of course, I've seen *Pygmalion* about twenty-five times. That's the connection between the actors and the audience, and you're right there. And, you know, in *The Dead*, John Huston also got it. You almost felt you were there, and it was like theatre."

21

Storm Warnings

Movies nearing the end of their production schedules rush around like squirrels trying to store food for the winter: a day here, half a day there, a second unit rushing off at odd hours to catch sunsets and drive-bys. Like Theophilus North, the movie company moved into the YMCA, but only for a week. In this old structure, cleverly doubling as an actual YMCA, Theophilus North's residential scenes will be shot. Just a block away from the Y, art director Eugene Lee outfitted a vacant store into a dusty barroom/pool hall where North will hang out with the servants and glimpse the underside of the moneyed lives with which he has been otherwise mingling.

The production had been running ahead of schedule, but rains have come to sunny Newport and driven the filming indoors. Ordinarily, films are planned to include indoor "cover sets" that can be used when exterior shooting is weathered out. Fortunately, the Y is also where Roberto Silvi has his editing room, so Danny was able to hop from working with the actors in one room to conferring with Silvi in another.

The scene to be shot is North being mobbed by townspeople who have come to his residence begging him to cure them of their ills with his magical static electricity. They are the same folks who will cheer his exoneration outside the courthouse in the scene filmed two weeks earlier. North hears of the reception committee when the YMCA desk clerk, played by playwright Christopher Durang (*Beyond Therapy*), nervously advises him of the friendly but pushy mob. Durang is a friend of producer Steven Haft who, coincidentally, produced the film version of *Beyond Therapy* that was directed by Robert Altman. Durang happened to be in Newport visiting Haft when Haft impressed him into service as an actor.

Also visiting the set was writer and animal rights activist Cleveland Amory, who was similarly tapped to perform a cameo as a former servant whose memory, but not his élan, is fading. Amory's recent profile of John Huston ran in the nationally circulated *Parade* Sunday supplement magazine.

Playing the kid brother of Elspeth Skeel was Hunter Carson, the young son of writer-director L.M. "Kit" Carson. He previously played Harry Dean Stanton's son in *Paris, Texas*. The world gets smaller and smaller. Adding to the "family" tradition on Huston pictures was Andy Bick, the son of Heritage Entertainment executive Jerry Bick and Oscar®-winning actress Louis Fletcher (Nurse Ratched in *One Flew Over the Cuckoo's Nest*). Bick flew in from Los Angeles in the hope of pulling enough strings to earn his Screen Actors Guild card. A SAG card requires a speaking role in a film, and when Bick shouted, "He's free!" as North flees the YMCA, he crossed from amateur to professional. Then he stayed on as a production assistant to wrangle the crowd scenes.

Even Joe Brooks got back into makeup for an "in joke" cameo (honoring his *F-Troop* role as the nearsighted lookout) as a blind man who claims to have been cured by North's static charge. When not acting, Brooks tallied up his schedules, call sheets, release forms and production records in his regular role as assistant director.

At the other end of the street, the *ad hoc* barroom and pool hall was seeing some action, preparing for the continuation of the shoot once the weather cleared. Little more than fifteen feet wide and thirty feet long, it was chock full of what art director Lee called "mood." "We didn't have to build all of it," he marveled. "We found an old wooden bar top, turned up a couple of wooden ice chest covers, and these old shelves. We'll probably keep the walls just like they are. After all, this isn't supposed to be fancy."

It certainly was not. In fact, it looked disgusting, just the sort of place to provide counterpoint to the Mahogany and brass elegance of the rich people's haunts. The bar was clearly working class and served admirably to underscore Wilder's observation of social and economic disparity during the Jazz Age. One of Lee's most subtle touches was a stack of newspapers dated 1926 complete with headlines and stories, illustrations and advertisements, including a classified notice for "T. Theophilus North, teacher" buried in the back section.

"Nobody will ever see it," Lee admitted, "but *we* know it's there. It all helps."

The fake papers lay at the end of the bar. Sales slips were spiked next to the cash register (all dated July and August, 1926), and antique liquor bottles stood at attention along the dusty shelves, interspersed with old-fashioned signs.

Three young Newport teenagers passed the storefront, then doubled back to look inside in wonderment at the Hollywood craftsmanship. The sight was so radically different from their computer-bred, high-tech adolescence that it must have been shocking—a step back in time and place that even these young people, and probably their parents, could never have known.

Time past, as well as time passed, are two sides of the same problem coin on a film set. Boredom crawls with the territory. It is not that anybody purposely wastes time; it is just that filmmaking is so complicated that it takes seemingly forever to do anything. This is why the actors, who, by the nature of their jobs, have to wait for everything to be in place before they can perform, while away the long hours reading, knitting, doing needlepoint, crossword puzzles, writing books, or phoning their agents. Mostly phoning their agents.

At The Breakers on another day, a number of actors, this time portraying servants, filled the languid time between set-ups by telling war stories. Richard Woods, Arnie Cox, Joe Gropper, and Patricia Beatson, decked in formal black and white uniforms, circa the 1920s, recalled the tricks they use finding work, not as servants, but as players, with the time-honored audition process. They swap stories about how to impress casting directors.

"You'll see actors coming in with their resumes," said Woods, who has played Henry James on television, where he was spotted by Steven Haft, and cast as Willis, the Bosworths' imperious butler. "They all say they studied here, or that so-and-so graduated *cum laude* from wherever. But one thing is: don't put where you studied or where you graduated from. Nothing puts someone off more than that. You're better off putting nothing down."

"They're hoping someone will recognize the name of their teacher and owe them a favor," suggested Patricia Beatson, playing a maid.

Arnie Cox, appearing as a gardener and footman, agreed. "I know one actor, he was so bad, he even listed his *auditions*."

"It comes under the heading of 'talent,'" proclaimed Joe Gropper, who, until turning to acting, was a Boston art dealer. "The casting people are usually friendly. They want you to succeed. In the beginning, when I was first starting out, it was personal and depressing if I didn't make it. Now it's different. They say that the average is twenty auditions before you get a job. It's the law of averages."

Joked Cox, "it's not a cattle *call*, it's a cattle *drive*." Cox attained visibility through television commercials for a bank in which he had to play basketball with the boy portraying his son. He reported that the shoot did not go well.

"I say (in the commercial), 'Hi. He's going to college and we have a way to pay for it.' We're tossing a ball and I'm supposed to take the ball away from him. On the first take, he doesn't want to give it to me. Next time, I come down and I take the ball, but I hit the rug, the rug slips out from under me, and I fall down. I go back, come down again, I get through it and flip the ball to the kid, and he's supposed to catch it. Instead, he just sits there and it hits him smack in the face." Cut and print. No good? Hardly. "I've been getting residuals for a couple of years from that!" Cox gloated.

Woods was more pragmatic. "You hit cycles," the distinguished actor said. "I was very hot three or four years ago, really hot. I had seven or eight commercials running at once. Then they get sick of your face for a while and you cool off. Then you start again. I did a toilet paper commercial, I can't mention the brand name, where I played the manager of a hotel showing a newlywed couple into an elaborate suite. Of course, in those days you couldn't show a *toilet*, but you could show the toilet *paper*. And they have nine rolls of toilet paper on this wall! I said, in my dialogue, 'Of course, in the Imperial Suite, we feature the entire line of X bathroom tissue.'" Woods said how, first, he, then the actress playing the newly married wife, and then the commercial's director, all broke into unstoppable giggles over the ridiculous surfeit of toilet paper but no john to put it in.

"The [client] ran out and I thought I was fired. Finally, I called my agent and said, 'Look, I just made a complete and total ass of myself.' But they used it, and I made a fortune, even though it was the most absolutely terrible commercial."

The days are gone when appearing in a commercial was a comedown in status. Still, Woods was careful.

"I won't do laxatives or anything that has to do with dentures," he decreed. "I'll do the commercial if I wasn't the one who had the dentures, but it's just the way I feel. And I won't do Santa Claus because you never make any money on it and you're so uncomfortable because you're all done up in all that *shmata*."

Woods learned from Steven Haft that he was the producer's first choice for the role. He said, "That's nice," and added, "but what I really wanted to ask was, 'how come you made me read for it again?' But it made me feel very good."

Joe Gropper turned to acting as a second profession. "When I came in for my call, there were thirty people, all together. I'm just a beginner, so using me was great. I'm just starting, and here I am, waiting around"—he nodded toward the stars—"just like the big guys."

Joe Brooks, his paperwork finished for the moment, joined the others to add his forty years' experience in the profession.

"I was an extra in the 40s, during the war, just out of high school," he recounted. "Most of the guys were in the service. I'd be working at Warners as a German in the morning, call Central Casting, and be over at Fox as an American soldier in the afternoon." He settled at the Goldwyn Studios for $1.04 an hour ("It was good money") but it was not until 1944's *The Fighting Seabees* that he won his first speaking part.

"It was for Republic Studios. I went in as an extra and they gave me a script and said to go to dinner. I drove over to Beverly Hills and told my girlfriend, 'I got a line. That's $35!' He recreated the scene. "So I'm in the cockpit of a plane and I've got to find a place to land. Then came my line: 'Roger.'

"That was it. When the show came out, you see the stock footage, you see the plane, and you see me go 'Wham!'" He paused to reflect. "You know, I watch it on TV and sometimes my line's cut out, and sometimes it's not. But it was $35. No residuals."

One aspect of Brooks' assistant director job was deciding which extras and bit players would be released, and which would be called back the next day to finish their scenes. With the company moving back and forth between filming at the YMCA and at The Breakers, it became a balancing act. The producers wanted to stay within budget, and the actors wanted to go to their next jobs.

The next day was Friday, August 28. Mitchum had departed, Grimes and her bumblebee had long since buzzed back to Manhattan, and Ernie Anderson had returned to California to wrap up the rest of his press agent work.

The rain began, and fell relentlessly on the sunny resort town, equally upon the rich and poor, with little indication of letting up.

22

Give 'em Hell

Director John Huston died at 2 AM Friday morning, August 28 in his sleep, while in Newport, Rhode Island. His death was caused by complications resulting from emphysema. He was 81 years old. He will be buried in Los Angeles. His family and many of his closest colleagues were with him over the past several weeks in connection with the filming of his script, *Theophilus North*, being directed by his son, Danny.

The official statement, released by the production company, gave the cold but effective notice of the passing of a legend. It said everything that needed to be said, and anything else would be added as time went on.

The news, while no surprise, was still shocking, and its weight fell mightily upon the shoulders of Danny and Anjelica Huston who were compelled by the pressures of their job to keep working. At the same time, they needed to be alone with him.

There was also something else, something the press release did not disclose: John Huston did not die in his sleep.

A month later, speaking before a capacity crowd honoring her father at the Directors Guild in Los Angeles, Anjelica set the record straight:

"On that last night, I think he knew pretty well where he was going— or maybe not *where* he was going, but *that* he was going."

Requesting that his family not see him in his final hours, he asked that only Maricela Hernandez be with him. As he lay dying, he assumed the part of a cavalry officer, perhaps like José Olimbrada, the Colonel under whom he had studied dressage when he joined the Mexican army in his twenties:

"How many express rifles do we have?" he asked Maricela.

"Thirty, John," she answered.

"How 'bout ammunition, baby?"

"Oh, we got plenty of ammunition."

Then he held her hand aloft the way a victorious prize fighter would do—another of his youthful adventures—and said:

"Then give 'em hell."

He died in her arms.

It was four hours before the police were called, during which time (as later revealed by Laurence Grobel in *The Hustons*) Anjelica, Danny and Tony Huston, Tommy Shaw, Zoë Sallis and Steven Haft assembled at the house. Suspicious of the time gap and circumstances, the Rhode Island police unceremoniously took Maricela to the police station in handcuffs. She was released immediately after Haft informed police who she was. There was also an unconfirmed twist to this story, not in the Grobel book, that would account for the police's suspicion. It says that they saw a bottle of pills labeled "experimental" and asked Maricela what they were for. "I was told to give it to him," she is supposed to have responded, at which point she was taken away.

By 6 AM, word had spread to a stunned film industry and the condolences began arriving. It wasn't that his death was unexpected—everybody knew he was terminally ill— it was just that, having slipped through Death's grasp so many times, it was hard to accept that, when the end finally came, it was in a comfortable resort town, not the Congo, Morocco, Yugoslavia, Mexico, Finland, or any of the hostile locations where he had made his movies.

This was, after all, the man who had once had a loaded pistol held to his head by a marauder who had then pulled the trigger. Only sheer luck made it jam. He was a man who suffered respiratory collapse, heart disease, and once bragged about having smoked cigars while he had pneumonia. A man who outlasted a youthful boxing career, filmed World War Two documentaries on the front line in which soldiers were killed on camera, survived attacks from Mexican *banditos*, ate a Congo meal of "long pig" (later discovered to have been human flesh), and survived Jack L. Warner, *Annie*, and his fifth wife, whom he referred to as "the crocodile."

"He was a landmark in film history, a great friend, and I'll miss him very much," said Michael Caine, who made two films with Huston: *Victory* and *The Man Who Would Be King*.

Robert Loggia (*Prizzi's Honor*) offered, "Working with him was a unique experience for an actor. He worked with the cast like a master conducting a symphony. He generated a feeling of love and loyalty. I had the same devastating feeling when my father died; they both passed away from emphysema."

Such tributes were not new, just sadder. In the past he had been compared to Chaplin as a director, lauded by figures as diverse as Otto Preminger and Truman Capote, and praised for his grit and tenacity by studio chief Dore Schary, journalist Lillian Ross, and critic James Agee.

Lamenting her friend's death, and remarking on the way he took political stands despite pressure to keep silent, Lauren Bacall said, "He was *about* something."

But the highest and most passionate compliment came from his own twenty-five-year-old son, Danny. When Huston's death was disclosed, Danny drove to Sea Meadow where Anjelica, Tony, and Zoë had joined Maricela, and where Anthony Edwards joined them by 9 A. M. Then Danny went to the set where he told Robin Vidgeon and the others to keep working.

"He's doing no more than John Huston himself would have done," reported production executive Ken Reiner.

Inside the YMCA set, the cast and crew hugged each other and silently took their places. There were no tears. It was learned that Huston had, quite unannounced, visited the editing alcove the previous Monday after everybody but Danny and Silvi had left. The three men had watched the assembled footage and John had pronounced it "top notch."

Little lifted the burden of grief that suffused the company. They soon discovered that they were held prisoner in the building, not just by the pouring rain, but by a growing number of mourners, journalists, and hangers-on who craved any information.

Anthony Edwards got the brunt of the attention as the only "star" who was recognizable. "It's a tragedy," he said with grace. "This is the saddest day of the year."

Tommy Shaw, who had worked with Huston for 30 years, showed a complex mixture of grief, anger, and relief. "He was the original 'macho man,'" he barked. "You can tell by his films. I can't tell you how much he meant to me. He was a huge part of my life. Everything really good that happened to me in this business was caused by him." Shaw paused before adding, "It's for the best, you know. He hated that wheelchair. He hated being that way."

Janet Roach found herself in an even more conflicting position. As a member of Huston's film family, she wanted to join her co-workers to complete the film; as a former news producer, she felt compelled to offer facts to the press. As a compromise, she reminisced. "John had been ill for years," she began. "But he had seen all of his children get launched. That meant a lot to him. Anjelica won the Oscar® for *Prizzi's Honor* and that was a great moment to him. He came here and saw the dailies. I saw him Tuesday and he was pleased as punch that Danny was doin' him proud. Tony had written a script (*The Dead*) that John was very pleased with, and Alegra is in the London publishing business; she's great. John had done a tremendous amount for everyone he cared about.

"John had room in his heart for so many people of all kinds, and the fact that he had room for one more—me—without anyone else being short-changed was a wonderful quality. More people should have it.

"I saw him yesterday at the house. We went over some changes we'd made in the script. His last words to me were"—she lowers her voice to do her affectionate impression one last time— "'Very good, Honey.' When we were writing *Prizzi's Honor* and this script, I lived for those words."

Dying on a slow news day is a curse. The weekend Huston died, Philippine President Corazon Aquino announced that she would deal harshly with rebels who tried to topple her government. The airlines promised to be good and stop delaying scheduled flights. And Senator William Proxmire, the founder of the "Golden Fleece Award" for government waste, announced that he would not run for re-election. Important, but no "stop the presses."

So John Huston became the media buzz. John Huston, whose life story was titled *An Open Book*, would have his death prove equally inviting.

Ava Gardner, who had originally been considered for the Lauren Bacall role, phoned the Budget Motor Inn production office to offer sympathy and request details. Mickey Rooney added his comments to the mounting praise. Any reporters who dared show up at Sea Meadow were threatened by Dan Ferreira and his *ad hoc* security force.

When Zoë Sallis arrived to collect Danny from the set, she was tailed by cameras. Or, so they thought; it was really another woman who was acting as Sallis' decoy. Later she and Danny returned the way they had escaped the first time, through the back door of the Y.

John Huston had planned to return to California anyway on Friday, August 28. His business in Newport was finished, and he was hoping to get another picture together for January. Because he carried a canister of pressurized oxygen, the commercial airlines would not allow him to travel, so he and the producers had been forced to charter a private jet for the trip back to the coast.

On Friday, August 28, 1987, John Huston, a meticulous filmmaker who never overlooked any useful detail, did not let the plane go to waste.

23

Wrapping Up

The end of a film that is shooting on location is like a college dormitory when classes and exams end and the summer rolls around. Where there was once boisterous camaraderie, there is little to be found roaming the hallway except dust balls. Just as students melt away to their homes at the end of term, so do film crews leave a location in pieces long before the editor huddles with the director to decide that there's enough footage, and the production manager calls, "That's a wrap."

The actors are released as they complete their scenes, the office personnel attends to closing out accounts, and everybody calls home to leave flight arrival times with wives, husbands and lovers. Location romances end.

There are no yearbooks to sign. There are some tears and sworn promises to stay in touch, most of which are broken.

The one ritual that is never missed, however, is the wrap party. Thrown by producers eager to thank their cast and crew for working so hard during the preceding months (never mind that there may still be pick-ups and post-production to do back in L.A.), the irony is less important than the celebration. *Mr. North*'s wrap party was held before the film wrapped, but after the death of John Huston. Perhaps it was his wake.

On the evening of Monday, September 7, as everyone arrived at Rosecliff (the "Gatsby" cottage) for revelry, most had to leave early so that they could be back on set the next morning. Tammy Grimes had returned from New York for retakes; her introductory scenes with Anthony Edwards were ruined by technical glitches. This had been discovered on the third day of filming but could not be rescheduled until now. Grimes and

Edwards, though inconvenienced, were extraordinarily lucky; very few actors get to re-shoot their important early scenes after they have had the opportunity to get to know their characters.

Harry Dean Stanton and Virginia Madsen, who just appeared together in the movie *Slam Dance*, also remained to join the party. Robin Vidgeon and his family returned to Rosecliff for the first time since *The Great Gatsby* 13 years earlier.

Shades of the film's first caterer, the ice man did not cometh for nearly an hour, and hot patrons were forced to chill their drinks in the mansion's fountains. Recorded music echoed through the ballrooms.

"It's not like in the old days," mused Paul Miller of the Preservation Society as he surveyed the collection of sport clothes and shorts on the guests who were eating barbecued finger food rather than elaborate canapés proffered to them by liveried servants. "In the old days, none of these people would be allowed in here dressed like this."

Also in the old days, actors would probably have had to use the servants' entrance.

Unwinding from the pressure of chauffeuring the now-departed Mitchum and Bacall, limousine owner Dan Ferreira took stock of some changes in Newport and the lack of others. "It's nothing to spend $50,000 for a wedding," he said, adding that he got his blueblood jobs strictly on referrals. "It costs $3,000 to $3,500 just for a mansion. I did a birthday party last winter where the man gave his wife everything, and the last gift of the night was a Jaguar!"

Would the Astors and Vanderbilts cut the same kind of rugs if they were around today?

"It's a lot of new money," Ferreira said, "but the style is coming back. When the mansions were built, there was no air conditioning, and for no amount of money could you buy a cool evening. Still, everyone tried to outdo each other. Husbands gave away diamonds as gifts; they brought in stone masons from Italy and gardeners from Holland. People here still pay attention to money. That's why I'll sometimes drive a Bentley: it's for the victor who doesn't want to wear the laurels."

And then there is Hollywood.

"Everyone wants to be near movies," Ferreira says. "They close their eyes and walk through that ballroom, and it all becomes real."

No one seemed more impressed by the effect than production executive Ken Reiner, who, having recently arrived from Los Angeles, was struck by the production's spirit of community. Perhaps he was referring to the audacity of Anthony Edwards offering to perform his own stunts. "A car chase without the cars" is how Robin Vidgeon described it, in which North, pursued by the townspeople who want him to "shock" them into health, flees for his life into a boat held for him by Harry Dean Stanton.

"We shot a chase through the town last Wednesday where the people follow North through the town to the docks, and watch him escape in a boat. They all wind up on the pier and some of them had to jump in the water. The water just *reeked*, and these people jumped into it *six times*! We'd keep saying, 'Be careful, be careful,' but the people in front would be hit by people behind them, and they'd all go in like the Keystone Kops. They never copped an attitude to it; that's the way these people are. It's not vanity. These people sincerely feel a part of the production."

The melee was also the occasion for one of those pranks that enliven the dailies: between scenes, Danny and Vidgeon had to relieve themselves into the water, and did so over the edge of the pier and out of sight. Or so they thought. Camera operator Stephen Shank and camera assistant Michael Endler had an unobstructed view and caught the cascade on film. At Thursday night's dailies, Danny and Robin won applause for their number one performances.

Other than that, the mood of the production was low-key; the people were still shaken by Huston's death.

As also happens, when one job winds down, people started searching for their next one. Roach was about to begin *In Her Own Image*, the Anna Murdoch book she adapted for a shoot in Australia in early 1988, "Where it's still summer."

Edwards: "Will it be good?"

Roach: "It *has* to be good."

Edwards: "*Mr. North* had something that most movies don't have. A good script."

Roach: "David Warner is a surprise. He did so much with Dr. McPherson."

Edwards: "And, of course, Theophilus North."

Roach: "You're in every scene for a reason."

Edwards: "I set you up to give me a great compliment and what happens?"

Edwards feigned offense and walked away, leaving Roach to swirl her glass of punch. "Do you know, whenever I got stuck about who Theophilus North was, I thought about Danny Huston. He's such a combination of traits. What would Danny do? That's the secret we had."

She also confided, at last, that Huston was more in contact with the production than anybody knew. "He saw dailies and saw some of the cut pieces of the film and pronounced himself very pleased," she offered quietly. "His hand is very much in this project, and certainly on the script. I'm sorry he died. But I'm sorriest for me, because I can't have the experience of writing with him again."

24

The Detail Work

A rthur "Skip" Steloff was just about to fall asleep under a huge shade tree on the lawn of Chateau-Sur-Mer, about 200 feet from where his money was being spent. He pushed his official Boston Red Sox cap over his eyes, allowing his grey, curly hair to puff out all around the edges of the dark blue fabric. For almost six weeks, *Mr. North* had been draining the cash reserves of Steloff's Heritage Entertainment, a feisty production and distribution firm which the former Navy man founded in 1966.

"We caught a comet by the tail," he said with the amazement more of a film fan than a film producer. "Anything out of John's head now has a life of its own, so in that respect we did, if you can call it luck, get lucky and inadvertently hook into that comet." That said, he remained pragmatic about distribution plans for what is, after all, a modest movie. "There won't be any one thousand or two thousand print breaks," he said, explaining that the cost of making a film doesn't end when the cameras stop rolling. Prints, advertising, and distribution costs can equal what is been spent to date. Not set up to handle those chores itself, Heritage was shopping the film to an outside distributor.

"We've got all kinds of offers from *everybody*, and now, with the new ancillary rights market becoming larger, *in toto*, than the entire theatrical market itself, it gives the independent guy like me a life where, ordinarily, I'd have been sitting and waiting. Studios have historically put all those rights (video, international, merchandising, etc.) together. I always had a strong background in splitting up those rights.[1]

---

1. Since then, of course, the ancillary market has dramatically changed with the killing of VHS and DVD and the emergence of Blu-Ray and, particularly, streaming delivery.

"My thinking is that no young guy should ever talk about making a picture until he's been in distribution; get out and find out what happens to a picture, and then you'll know the film business. Then, when you're a distributor, go stand in front of a theatre and watch what that theatre owner does to the distributor. And then you'll know what that mystical, magical thing called 'cash flow' is."[2]

The attitude of the major studios with whom Steloff had spoken up to this point made him cringe. "When we first took this to the studios, they called it a 'special' picture, meaning 'limited appeal.' I said, 'Was *On Golden Pond* special? Was *Room with a View* special?' It's like they have an argument list and as soon as you hit one, they say, 'Gotcha!' The hindsight game is marvelous."

It was Steven Haft who brought *Mr. North* to Steloff, and he happened upon the project almost by accident. "I was in Newport in 1980 for a film on the America's Cup," the 30-ish, scholarly looking Haft recalled. "I'd heard about the book *Theophilus North* from a friend who liked it, but I didn't get around to optioning it until 1984. After I had acquired the book, I learned that another producer had had a script written and that the book had a life of its own, and fans. First you find a stray dog, and then you discover that it has a pedigree." Budding producer Haft, who was already involved with bringing Christopher Durang's *Beyond Therapy* to the screen, knew at once whom to cast as Bosworth in *Mr. North*. "The first person I ever saw in my mind in this movie was John Huston," Haft remembered. But landing Huston or any star cast proved as elusive as the financing. "*Beyond Therapy* not only gave me a producing credit but it put me in touch with Danny Huston's agents. They offered me Danny Huston as director. Danny read it, called John, short-circuited the agents, and they began to focus on it."

"There were never less than twenty companies interested in the film at any point," Haft continued, adding that no studio would actually commit; all they did was take meetings. "Multiply three excuses and the four new corporate levels you have to go through times twenty companies and that's every day's work. As I was sitting there through eighty calls a day, I kept imagining it would have been easier to get a slasher picture together."

---

2.   Theatres, all told, keep about half of a film's theatrical gross, and everybody down the line must recoup his percentage from whatever is left after the distributor takes a share, pays off advertising and prints, etc. The old formula used to be that it takes 2.8 times the cost of a film to break even. In practice, very few movies break even, ever, which is not to say that they don't make money.

That is when Haft met Steloff. In 1959, former television executive Steloff realized that there was a future in licensing old movies and TV shows to local stations who were desperate for programming but couldn't afford to produce their own. This came to be known as "syndication," and it represented the most lucrative end of the business, for it is what finally put series and movies into profits.

By 1969 Steloff and Heritage had gone public and, by 1982, had diversified into production as a hedge against exponentially increasing syndication licensing costs. Revenues in 1986 were $25 million, not huge by Hollywood standards; the American film industry grossed $4.2 *billion* in 1987, and gazillions more since then, but strong enough to inspire Steloff to launch a slate of pictures. One of them was to be *Mr. North*.

Haft: "They got the script on a Friday and I got a call on Monday asking if I could be in Los Angeles on Tuesday at 4:30. They didn't send me a ticket, however."

He flew out from New York anyway, and it wound up being a short meeting. "Within minutes of meeting Skip," Haft remembered, "he said, 'We're going to make this picture.'"

With the Hustons' names attached, even more began to happen. Everybody in town wanted to take part in *Mr. North*, most agreeing to work far below their traditional salaries just to be part of it.

"We hope to avoid the people who won't talk to us unless there's seven figures," says Ken Reiner, a former United Artists production executive who joined Steloff during Heritage's expansion. "We don't want to deal with 'Hollywood.' A film like *Mr. North* has the sort of insights into human nature that you don't get in *Rambo*. It's something of an heirloom picture."

Perhaps prescient that his film would face a tough theatrical market, Steloff was hoping to be bailed out by ancillary rights (home video, cable, airline, etc.). "Ancillary markets have opened up a world," he enthused at the time. "If you have the backing and the knowledge, both of which you can achieve, you can get into those ancillary markets and do well. Lots of pictures are rented today on home video not because they're enjoyed, but because they got great publicity. They're rented on the basis of how much exposure they've had in other media, especially theatrical. But before a good video release can be achieved, you have to open that picture in a minimum of twenty to thirty markets, a minimum of several hundred theatres, and run it for a certain length of time with a certain number of prints.[3]

"It's the great game, the eternal chase," Steloff said, shifting his position beneath the chestnut tree to follow the shade. He cites such founding moguls as Samuel Goldwyn, Louis B. Mayer, Harry Cohn, and Jack L. Warner, noting their cutthroat ways which ruined lives and careers while creating film art and iconography.

"I don't think it's the ego," he said. "It's the love of it. It's the incredible moment at which the dream becomes real: when people actually plop down their ticket money. That's the payoff to a gamble that you've bet and won, because; guess what, you took a chance a year before."

---

3. Update: In this century, video revenues have dwindled as the cost of making and marketing films has risen and the threat of piracy has eroded revenues. Immediate worldwide openings is the only way thus far devised to counter this trend, but ancillary markets continue to suffer as filmmaking costs rise.

25

End Notes

Thornton Wilder wrote, in his Pulitzer Prize-winning play, *Our Town*, that the most revealing aspects of human life are the ones to which people pay the least attention. The world is formed, Wilder held, not by the momentous occasions of history, but by slight, subtle daily incidents. In *Our Town* he built an entire play around them, finding profundity in minutiae. In *The Bridge of San Luis Rey*, a novella which won him another Pulitzer Prize, he explored the same theme of how the smallest details can lend weight to matters of Fate. In many ways, *Theophilus North* covers the same area, albeit later in Wilder's contemplative life. It is a novel of incident, of description, and of nuance.

Details are similarly important to filmmakers. Every motion picture is constructed of individual shots, but each shot is a tapestry of costume, color, light, background, movement, face, makeup, prop, word, and expression. Watching a film, it is easy to forget that, until somebody decided to place something in front of the camera, the screen was blank. Even before that, until a writer put thoughts into words, the page was, likewise, blank.

Mr. North is not a classic film, or a financially successful one, or one that changed the art of cinema. But therein may be found its importance. As Wilder wrote, it is the small things that define life. The people who came together for six weeks to shoot a movie, and the ways in which each was affected by the man who drew them together, yet never saw their finished work, are only one example of what happens every time a camera turns. It is the craft, it is what it takes, and it is what you do. Sometimes it works, more often it does not, and nobody really knows going in which it will be. So, the experience itself becomes the reward; it has to.

In the many television tributes to John Huston that followed his death, news programs ran clips from his best-remembered movies, invariably starting with *The Maltese Falcon*. Pathetically, the most widely circulated clip of that film was taken from a "colorized" version of this black and white classic, a bastardization of his art that Huston, even in failing health, had denounced in a celebrated taped statement to a Congressional committee on the rights of artists. Through his efforts, as well as those of Martin Scorsese, Woody Allen, Sydney Pollack, and others, the National Film Registry was established to, among other things, assure the preservation of the original versions of a director's work and to label anything that veers from it.

Throughout the filming of *Mr. North*, the press had consistently, and wrongly, reported that Jack Nicholson, then Anjelica Huston's longtime partner, had been staying in nearby Providence, Rhode Island, keeping her company. The fact that nobody had actually seen him (he was in Los Angeles the whole time) didn't bother anybody. The rumors had become even more malicious when it was reported that John Huston, on his deathbed, made Nicholson promise to marry his daughter, which was also false.

Of course, if people weren't curious about Huston and *Mr. North*, that would also have been a problem. Given the pressure of production and his health, it became that rare film that actually had to decline publicity.

In December of 1987 the final film that Huston himself directed, *The Dead*, was released theatrically. It garnered larger box office revenues and received more appreciative reviews than any of his films in the previous ten years. At the end of its opening titles, following the credit "Directed by John Huston,"—comes the dedication: "for Maricela."

Epilogue

Heritage sold *Mr. North* to the Samuel Goldwyn Company, who had expertise in handling "special" (sic) pictures, for distribution. Lacking the clout of a major distributor, Goldwyn was at a disadvantage in securing choice bookings and settled for a July 22, 1988 American theatrical debut. It entered a marketplace that was eighty-five percent controlled by the studios, leaving fifteen percent for independents. It has become worse since then, or better, if you happen to be a studio. It received gently appreciative reviews, some of which focused on John Huston, and thereafter made its way onto Virgin Visions home video for VHS and laserdisc release. Some time later, the film's theatrical rights were acquired by MGM/UA, and the DVD rights to a rights aggregation company called "Media Favorites" that is handled by Amazon.com.

Just before its original theatrical release, Danny Huston returned to Newport and Boston to speak with the press. Once he had finished the obligatory interviews, he stretched his lanky then-26-year-old form onto a couch at Boston's Four Seasons hotel and let his mind roll back to the previous summer. Strangely, although we had been in contact throughout the entire six-week shoot, we had never sat down for a full formal interview or even, for that matter, to simply chew the fat. When he was shooting, I was taking notes, and when he was editing or screening dailies, I was writing my *Herald* stories and commuting between Newport and Boston.

"I don't want to sound presumptuous," he said, "but I feel that I am carrying on a dynasty. I am a Huston and I have to treat this gift carefully, rather than just exploit it." He lit a cigarette, ignoring the fact that tobacco helped kill his father less than a year earlier, and reminisced about how the "glorious adventure" played out. "A lot of people have been asking me if it was hard working with actors of the caliber of Mitchum, Bacall, Stanton, Grimes, and the others," he offered. "Really, it isn't. You read the dialogue over and over to yourself and try to hear it, but then you give it to Bacall and it's like magic. What's so difficult about that? you then think. So working with veterans, giants of that kind, really makes the job very easy.

"There were a lot of colorful and varied characters which would not only attract a strong cast but would give me the opportunity to create all of these totally different characters of different ages and classes." As for putting big stars in small roles, he explained, "They read the script in which the dialogue was good, and they saw that they could give a good performance. It's not something they come by that often. They might have had bigger parts [elsewhere], but they're not working with this kind of material. And, of course, my father being attached to the project gave it a certain amount of weight it wouldn't otherwise have had."

Did the restricted budget alter the way he wanted to shoot? "Not really," he said, his mind scrolling back to make sure. "I like working under low budget conditions. I like not being able to go back and re-shoot; I don't think people should have that liberty. I think you've got to get things right the first time and, if you don't, well, you've got to live with your mistakes and make sure you never do it again. It turns out very much how I thought it would. The only thing that saddens me is not having my father in there, but that's because he's my father. Mitchum did a great job and I'm forever grateful."

Looking at the film again, it becomes apparent that Mitchum's character was not called upon to move out of his chair, except in one instance, in the courtroom scene.

"I shot it and approached it as if Mitchum was Dad," Danny revealed. "Thinking back, it would have been the same because my father couldn't get around all that quickly, and that's the way I would have filmed my father. And thank God my father didn't do it, because that would've been a nightmare: [the courtroom] was so hot, it would have been a very difficult scene for him to do."

At the time of the interview, Danny was mulling several future projects. He wasn't bothered that offers hadn't come flooding in. "I work not because I have this incredible need to express this artistic flow which I have inside of me. I need the money, and it's something that I do professionally. It's a craft. So money is a factor, but I can't sell myself, especially now. Maybe in a few years." Yet, he was also deflecting persistent inqui-ries about whether he, brother Tony, and sister Anjelica would try to work together. The rumors were fueled by word that sister Alegra had discov-ered a literary property that seemed tempting as a family affair. "All the elements would have to be just right," Danny said, a leading smile rising on his face. "My father always told me that the story is the most important thing, not getting the family together."

Since 1988

Danny Huston directed sporadically since *Mr. North*. His credits include *Becoming Colette* in 1991 and *Ice Princess* for HBO in 1995. Starting in 1997 he began to specialize in acting, winning increasing acclaim for a wide range of portrayals from Stiva in *Anna Karenina* (1997) to *X-men Origins: Wolverine* (2009). From 1989 to 1992 he was married to Virginia Madsen. In 2002 he married Katie Jane Evans, with whom he had a child. The couple was going through divorce proceedings in 2008 when Evans took her own life.

After *Mr. North* and *Prizzi's Honor*, Janet Roach wrote the television film on the Three Stooges and scripted several Nero Wolfe mysteries. She taught writing at Columbia University School of the Arts and is currently writing *Swimming with Dinner*, an adventure novel set in New Zealand where she and her husband dwelled for a time.

Anthony Edwards became a major television star in the role of Dr. Mark Greene from 1994 to 2008 on the hit series *E.R.* He has continued to act in television and films and, while not an above-the-title star, delivers solid and winning character performances.

Robert Mitchum died in 1997 of complications from lung cancer and emphysema.

Lauren Bacall made occasional appearances in movies and TV, increasingly as a highly recognizable voice talent. In 2006 she published *By Myself and Then Some*, the continuation of her 1979 memoir, *By Myself*. She died in 2014 at age 89.

Harry Dean Stanton appeared in the films *Fear and Loathing in Las Vegas* and *The Mighty*. Director Drago Sumonja's 2009 documentary *Character* offers a fascinating profile of him, and he plays Monday nights in a musical group in Los Angeles.

Anjelica Huston married actor Robert Graham in 1992 (he died in 2008) and continued to act in films. She made her directing debut in 1996 with *Bastard Out of Carolina*. In addition to those films cited earlier, she has moved into character roles with *Buffalo 66, Material Girls,* and other films.

Mary Stuart Masterson has continued acting and made *The Florentine, The Book of Stars* and *Benny & Joon*. In 2003 she began producing with *Last Man Running* and directing in 2006 with *The Insurgents*.

Virginia Madsen appeared in *The Haunting* and *John Grisham's The Rainmaker*. She received well-deserved acclaim for 2004's *Sideways*.

Tammy Grimes has appeared sporadically in films, including *High Art* and *Trouble in the Corner*. In 2003 she was inducted into the American Theatre Hall of Fame and has since turned her talents into a one-woman show.

David Warner is a frequent character presence in films, most notably in James Cameron's, *Titanic*. He continues to essay character roles with superb skill, and in 2001 returned to the London stage after several decades' absence to act in *Major Barbara*. In 2013 he appeared notably in an episode of *Doctor Who*.

Mark Metcalf has been seen on television in guest roles in such series as *Teen Angel* and *Buffy the Vampire Slayer*. In 2000, he left Hollywood for Michigan and began working in children's theatre.

Christopher Lawford has continued to appear in numerous films including *Dead Broke, Witness to the Mob, Thirteen Days,* and *Kiss Me, Guido*. He now writes and does charity work to help recovering addicts (www.christopherkennedylawford.com).

Joe Brooks, before his death in 2007, was a popular guest at celebrity conventions where fans lined up to meet the former *F-Troop* lookout.

Steven Haft's next film after *Mr. North* was *Dead Poets Society* which was nominated for the Best Picture Academy Award® and won the Best Original Screenplay Oscar® for Tom Schulman. Haft became one of Hollywood's most prestigious independent producers with credits such as *Pirates of Silicon Valley, Emma,* and *The Singing Detective*.

Karen Golden continues as one of the industry's busiest and most respected script supervisors, having worked on such films as *Bull Durham, White Men Can't Jump, Blue Chips,* and *Mystery Men* before starting collaboration with Michael Bay on the *Transformers* series.

Tom Shaw continued as an active Unit Production Manager and DGA member for several years following *Mr. North*. His daughter, Ann, gave birth to a son, also named Tommy, after production wrapped.

Roberto Silvi works constantly as film editor in Italy and America. His credits include *Tombstone, Twister*, and two films for Danny Huston, *Becoming Colette* and *The Maddening*.

Robin Vidgeon has photographed film and television, chiefly in the UK, such as *Neverending Story III, Breaking the Code*, and the mini-series *Tilly Trotter*.

Ann Dollard, Danny Huston's and Christopher Lawford's agent, was killed in July, 1988 in a horseback riding accident. The popular Dollard's death not only sent shockwaves of grief through the industry, it triggered a series of mergers, shifts, and personnel changes among Hollywood's talent agencies that continues.

Ernie Anderson passed away in 1995 of heart failure at the age of 85.

The Author moved to Los Angeles in 1993 to produce television documentaries and write books, among other things.

Theophilus North
by Thornton Wilder
(Synopsis)

If there is a thematic continuity to Thornton Wilder's writing, it is optimism leavened with reality—neither the Pollyanna optimism of Horatio Alger nor the biting Candidian satire of Voltaire, but a sense that, despite life's curves, there is an ultimate trajectory. His major works embody this duality. The studied banality on the surface of *Our Town* (1938), for example, asks us to see how so much of what we take for granted is worthy of closer appreciation. *The Skin of Our Teeth* (1942), with its circus-like vision of the end of the human race, constantly begs audiences to ask why its characters cannot see what is clearly in front of them. *The Bridge of San Luis Rey* (1927), a mystery whose solution is ultimately that there is no solution, nevertheless calls for an exploration of why tragedies happen. Even in the screenplay for Alfred Hitchcock's bucolic murder story, *Shadow of a Doubt* (1942), in which black comedy mixes with genuine malice, Wilder's ear for darkness within the brightness produced a masterful blend that made it the director's favorite film.

Theophilus North, Wilder's last (1973) novel, is less distinguished than his earlier work. Nevertheless, it keeps its chin up, even though its phantasmagorical element, North's healing static charge, seems too slight a plot point on which to hang a dramatic climax. Whether North himself is an enigma or just cast in smoke depends on how the reader feels about relentlessly free spirits. According to Matthew Angelo, writing for the Thornton Wilder Society, the novel came about because Wilder, whose identical twin would have been named Theophilus, died an hour after he was born, wanted to write a memoir of his brother as if he had lived.[1]

---

1. Matthew Angelo, "Synopsis," the Thornton Wilder Society website (www. twildersociety.org).

The result is a picaresque novel that lent only a few of its many narrative threads to James Costigan's screenplay adaptation.[2] The story begins in 1926 as the eponymous character (Anthony Edwards) arrives in Newport, Rhode Island. In the book, it is because he has tired of his job as a New Jersey schoolteacher and longs to recapture the sense of wonderment that his Garden State students lacked. He also wants to pursue a bucket list of occupations that he feels will bring about fulfillment, among them magician, detective, romantic, and possible martyr. The film shows him quitting his job as a private tutor to a trio of obnoxious homunculi ("Madame, I suggest you urge your children to play with matches") and pedal off on his bicycle.

He arrives in Newport and applies for work at the home of James McHenry Bosworth (Robert Mitchum). Bosworth's arch daughter, Sally Baily-Lewis (Tammy Grimes), takes time to berate her maid, Sally (Sarah) Boffin (Virginia Madsen), then hires North to read scripture to her invalid father for two hours a day, twice a week for a reluctantly yielded two dollars an hour. Bosworth is incontinent and housebound, two conditions that his daughter and her sleazy consulting physician Dr. Angus McPherson (David Warner) are in no hurry to relieve. During the interview, North espies Mrs. Bailey-Lewis' widowed daughter, Persis Bosworth-Tennyson (Anjelica Huston) and they exchange promising looks. North and Bosworth immediately bond, even though North went to Yale and Bosworth is a Harvard graduate, as they both recognize their adventurous, if not mutually scandalous, natures. North also discloses that he has the capacity to generate a static electric charge that conveys a slight shock when he touches people.

Because North enters the Bosworth home through the front door, he is not permitted, by tradition, to room in the boarding house of Mrs. Amelia Crandall (Lauren Bacall), whose facilities are reserved for servants, so he billets himself at the local YMCA. In due course, he meets Henry Simmons (Harry Dean Stanton), a cockney butler who, in truth, comes from Chicago and tells him that everybody in town is some kind of poseur. Even though he cannot stay there, North is welcome as a visitor at Crandall's hostelry, which also serves as a retirement home and hospice. It is here that he learns about the "death watch" by which the servants protect the lives of the town's elderly rich folks from mercenary heirs and the conniving Dr. McPherson.

---

2. In 2004, Wilder's novel was adapted for the stage by James Burnett. In 2006 it was performed at the Harold Clurman Theatre in New York.

North takes a variety of part-time jobs. As a children's tennis coach, he pauses to "shock" his young charges, to their squealing delight. While teaching French to young Elspeth Skeel (Mary Stuart Masterson), she confides to him that her migraine headaches have impelled her father (Mark Metcalf) and mother (Katharine Houghton), to follow Dr. McPherson's recommendation that she be sent to an asylum. She asks him to use his sparks on her as a cure; he does, and she swoons. When Mr. Skeel learns of this, he angrily bars North from giving his daughter further lessons.

While visiting a municipal office, North is taken aside by Sally Boffin who warns him that Mrs. Bailey-Lewis and Dr. McPherson are plotting to keep Bosworth a prisoner in his own mansion. North heads to the Bosworth home and uses ju-jitsu to overpower a newly hired guard and enters. He finds Bosworth and offers to find a way to take him out in public without embarrassment. He returns with a set of rubber pants and the two men enjoy an outing.

North encounters Sally Boffin once more at the town's Fourth of July parade. They tentatively begin to make out, but it's clear that she has her mind elsewhere. Indeed it is; she is already in a relationship with Boston scion Michael Patrick Ennis III (Chris Lawford), but she feels that their future is doomed because of their differing social stations. North impresses upon her that even the bluebloods are only one or two steps away from the old country and, besides, this is America. They part as friends.

That night North is summoned to the Skeel home where Elpeth has a migraine that Dr. McPherson insists cannot be cured. North cures it simply by respecting the young lady and giving her attention. He also helps Tanni Lislotte (Harriet Rogers), an ageing nanny living in Mrs. Crandall's boarding house, feel at peace before she passes over. Word spreads about North's "power" and, before long, townspeople flock to him at the YMCA to beg them to relieve their maladies. Enraged, Dr. McPherson swears out a warrant for North's arrest on charges of practicing medicine without a license. North flees both the rabble and the police in a comic chase but is captured.

At the inevitable trial before Judge Nicholas Cadwalader (Judge Thomas Needham), McPherson is humiliated when the Skeels reveal his incompetence, and Mrs. Crandall testifies in North's behalf, stressing he never took money for his cures, unlike McPherson who takes money and cures nothing. North demonstrates his harmless static abilities for the Judge and all charges, so to speak, are dismissed.

After the trial, North is invited to a season's climax ball where he is introduced to Mrs. and Mrs. Michael Patrick Ennis III—and it is Sally. Then

Sally is introduced to Mrs. Baily-Lewis, and Mrs. Bailey-Lewis goes batty. Enjoying watching all of this, and out of the house as well, Bosworth pulls North aside and offers to fund a philosophical and educational academy to broaden people's experience and open their minds. He happily accepts and soon spots Bosworth's granddaughter, Persis, looking at him across the crowded ballroom. The two of them finally approach each other and dance as sparks fly and the credits roll.

Mr. North (1988)
Cast and Credits

Directed by Danny Huston
Based on the novel *Theophilus North* by Thornton Wilder
Screenplay by John Huston & Janet Roach and James Costigan
Produced by Steven Haft and Skip Steloff
Executive Producer: John Huston
Cinematographer: Robin Vidgeon
Film Editor: Roberto Silvi
Casting: Risa Bramon Garcia, Billy Hopkins
Production Designer: Eugene Lee
Costume Designer: Rita Riggs

Cast:
Anthony Edwards: Theophilus North
Robert Mitchum: John McHenry Bosworth
Lauren Bacall: Amelia Cranston
Harry Dean Stanton: Henry Simmons
Anjelica Huston: Persis Bosworth-Tennyson
Mary Stuart Masterson: Elspeth Skeel
Virginia Madsen: Sally (Sarah) Boffin
Tammy Grimes: Sarah Baily-Lewis
David Warner: Doctor Angus McPherson
Hunter Carson: Galloper Skeel
Christopher Durang: YMCA Clerk
Mark Metcalf: Mr. Skeel
Katharine Houghton: Mrs. Skeel
Judge Thomas H. Needham: Judge Nicholas Cadwalader

Richard Woods: Willis
Harriet Rogers: Tanie Lislotte
Layla Sommers: Nadia Denby
Lucas Hall: Joseph Denby
Thomas-Laurence Hand: Luther Denby
Linda Peterson: Mrs. Denby
Cleveland Amory: Mr. Danforth
Christopher Lawford: Michael Patrick Ennis III
Albert A. Conti: Arresting Officer
Ellen Hamilton Latzen: Ada
Katherine Wiatt: Eloise
Jason Adams: Johnny
Arthur Bowen: Claybourne Tantamount
Marietta Tree: Amanda Venable
Richard Kneeland: Buster Venable
Alegra Huston: Miss Melmore
Barbara Blossom: YMCA Visitor
Mara Clark: YMCA Visitor
Belle McDonald: YMCA Visitor
Bill L. McDonald: YMCA Visitor
John Heeney McKay: YMCA Visitor
William A. Lynch: Bartender
David Kennett: Patron in Billiard Parlor
Richard McElvain: Patron in Billiard Parlor
Richard Seguin: Patron in Billiard Parlor
Frank Dolan: Patron in Billiard Parlor
Richard C. Snee: Patron in Billiard Parlor
Dick Durock: The Bouncer
Al Ruban: Court Clerk
Helen Gustafson: Courtroom Spectator
Ann Brennan: Courtroom Spectator
John Mulqueeney: Man on Porch #1
Martin H. Myers: Man on Porch #2
Geraldine LiBrandi: Nurse Chalmers
Jack McCullough: Warrant Officer
Arthur Skip Steloff: Mino Matera
Anna Severa: Rosa
Seth T. Walker: Runner #1
Helen A. Ksypka: Runner #2

Crew:

Produced in Association with Showcase Productions, International, Inc.

Executive in Charge of Production for Heritage Entertainment: Al Ruban

Music Supervision: Seth Kaplan for OSS

Production Manager: Tom Shaw

First Assistant Director: Anthony J. Cerdone

Second Assistant Director: John 'Joe' Brooks

Camera Operator: Steven Shank

First Assistant Camera: Michael Endler

Second Assistant Camera: Albert Malvaez

Steadicam Operator: John C MacNeil

Still Photographer: Anthony K. Roberts

Script Supervisor: Karen Golden

Production Executive: Ken Reiner

Production Coordinator Anne M. Shaw

Additional Production Coordinator: Patricia Raya-Macmillian

Production Secretary: Christine Altomari

Set Decoration: Sandra Nathanson

Researcher, Set Dresser: Randall Garrett Bliss

Scenic Artist: Kathleen Fillion

Prop Master: Robert H. Schleinig

Assistant Prop Master: Randi Savoy

Storyboard Artist: Jeff Ralsmeyer

Gaffer: Ross Maehl

Best Boy Electric: Philip Walker

Electricians: Frank Miranda, Robert Becchio, Elizabeth Hanson, Scott Drinon, Maureen Ryan, Alex Drought

Key Grip: Frank Keever

Best Boy Grip: Richard Lewis

Dolly Grip: William G. Kenney

Grips: Erich Augenstein, Philip Michelson, David Chapman, Stephen Girouard

Sound Mixer: William Randall, Sr. CAS

Boom Operator: William Randall, Jr.

Key Make-up: Robert Arrollo

Make-up Artist: Keis Maes

Special Make-up: Fern Buckner

Hairstylist:Frida Aradóttir
Special Hairstylist: Anthony Cortino
Assistant to Costume Designer: Deborah Newhall
Wardrobe Assistants: Ann S. Smith, Marilyn Salvatore, Suzanne
    Baldaia, Karen A. Gilbert, Steven Light
Post-Production Supervisor: Eric Barrett
Assistant Film Editors: Deborah Zeitman, Keith M. Sheridan
Apprentice Editor: Kevin W. Angeletti
Supervising Sound Editor: Tony Palk
Supervising Dialogue Editor: Marvin I. Kosberg
Sound Editor: Phil Haberman
Music Editors: Denis Ricotta, John Harris
Assistant Sound Editor: Karen Kory
Re-recording Mixers: Wayne Heitman, Matthew Iadarola
Sound Recordist: Jeanette Browning
Original music by David McHugh
Scoring Engineer: Armin Steiner
Scoring Crew: Walt Borchers, Terry Brown, Chuck Garsha
Source Music Engineers: Greg Townley, Nick Viterelli
Production Accountant—Newport: Diana Johnson
Production Accountant—L.A.: Susan Jensen
Stunt Coordinators: Michael Lee Baron, Warren A. Stevens
Transportation Coordinator: Ronnie Baker
Transportation Captain: Ronald H. Sweet
Drivers: Raymond J. Reall Sr., Lewis A. Perrotti, Peter Leone, Charles
    Scherra, Charles Stevens, Frederick R. Reed, Steven Reeves, James
    Vickers, Michael Amaral, Frank L. Calabro, Edward Baffori, John
    J. Meehan, Daniel Ferreira, Steve Anton, Allie Souza, Fylis
    Souza
Camera Operator: Jonathan Rasmussen
Antique Cars: Ted Leonard
Construction Supervisor: Michael McGarty
Carpenters: Christopher J. Kane, Brian Holland, James Hoxeng,
    Anthony Lindas, George A. Marcincavage
Painters: Sarah Burt, Alfred Chin, Joseph Celho, Jr., Terrence
    O'Leary, Jr., Shauna Sampson
Projectionists: Alan Jacques, Robert Santaniello
Assistant to Danny Huston: Marquerite de Pourtales
Assistant to the Producers: Jill Niemond, Doug Dempsey

Production Assistants—Newport: George T. Nelson, Danielle F. Ferreira

Location and Housings Liaison: Virginia Baldwin

Office Assistants—L.A.: Jeffrey Santoro, David Coffey

Intern: Diane Flanagan

Stand-Ins: Linda Maehl, William J. Norbury

Titles: Robert Dawson

Unit Publicist: Ernie Anderson

Production Counsel: George Sheanshang, Esq.

Location Casting: Ann Baxter

Police Officer: Albert Conti

Post-Production Facilities: JDH Sound, Inc.

Color Timer: Steve Sheridan

Ultra-Stereo Consultant: Bruce Weitz

Negative Cutter: Jim Sheridan

Running Time: 89 minutes

MPAA Rating: PG

Nat Segaloff
Biography

Nat Segaloff always wanted to write and produce, but it took him several careers before he learned how to get paid for it. He was a journalist for *The Boston Herald* covering the motion picture business, but has also at various times been a studio publicist (Fox, UA, Columbia), college teacher (Boston University, Boston College), on-air TV presenter (Group W), entertainment critic (CBS radio) and author (twelve books including *Hurricane Billy: The Stormy Life and Films of William Friedkin* and, as co-author, *Love Stories: Hollywood's Most Romantic Movies)*. He has contributed career monographs on screenwriters Stirling Silliphant, Walon Green, Paul Mazursky, and John Milius to the University of California Press' acclaimed *Backstory* series. His writing has appeared in such varied periodicals as *Film Comment, Written By, International Documentary, Animation Magazine, The Christian Science Monitor, Time Out* (US*), MacWorld*, and *American Movie Classics Magazine*. He was also senior reviewer for AudiobookCafe.com.

His *The Everything® Etiquette Book, The Everything Trivia Book,* and *The Everything® Tall Tales, Legends & Outrageous Lies Book,* went into multiple printings for Adams Media Corp. Other books include *Arthur Penn: American Director, Final Cuts: The Last Films of 50 Great Directors,* and *Stirling Silliphant: The Fingers of God* (the latter two for BearManor Media).

As a TV writer-producer, Segaloff helped perfect the format and created episodes for A&E's flagship *Biography* series. His distinctive episodes include "John Belushi: Funny You Should Ask"; "Shari Lewis & Lamb Chop"; "Larry King: Talk of Fame"; "Darryl F. Zanuck: Twentieth Century-Filmmaker" and "Stan Lee: The ComiX-MAN!" He has written and co-produced the *Rock 'n' Roll Moments* music documentaries for The Learning Channel/Malcolm Leo Productions, and has written and/ or produced programming for New World, Disney, Turner, and USA Networks. He is co-creator/co-producer of *Judgment Day* with Grosso-Jacobson Communications Corp. for HBO.

His extraterrestrial endeavors include the cheeky sequel to the Orson Welles "*Invasion From Mars*" radio hoax, "*When Welles Collide*," which featured a "*Star Trek*"* cast. It was produced by L.A. Theatre Works and has become a Halloween tradition on National Public Radio. In 1996 he formed the multi-media production company Alien Voices* with actors Leonard Nimoy and actor John de Lancie. Segaloff produced five best-selling, fully dramatized audio plays for Simon & Schuster: *The Time Machine, Journey to the Center of the Earth, The Lost World, The Invisible Man,* and *TheFirst Men in the Moon,* all of which feature "*Star Trek*"* casts. Additionally, his teleplay for *The First Men in the Moon* was the first-ever TV/Internet simulcast and was presented live by The Sci-Fi Channel. He has also written narrative concerts for the Los Angeles Philharmonic, celebrity events, is a script consultant, and was a contributing writer to *Moving Pictures* magazine.

Nat is the co-author with Arnie Reisman and Daniel M. Kimmel of *The Waldorf Conference*, a comedy-drama about the secret 1947 meeting of studio moguls that began the Hollywood Blacklist. Its all-star world premiere was at L.A. Theatre Works and was acquired for production by Warner Bros. He produced a subsequent production to benefit the Hollywood ACLU and the Writers Guild Foundation. Nat has also produced such other celebrity events as a public reading of censored books and a recreation of the classic anti-HUAC broadcast, *Hollywood Fights Back* called *Hollywood Fights Back… Again.* He was staff producer for The Africa Channel, wrote and co-directed with Callard Harris the dramatic short, *Devil's Run,* and has been a frequent special guest panelist on the NPR word/game show "*Says You!*"

He is currently writing the biography of award-winning writer Harlan Ellison.

Index

*Numbers in **bold** indicate photographs*

165

www.ingramcontent.com/pod-product-compliance
Lightning Source LLC
Chambersburg PA
CBHW070800100426
42742CB00012B/2203